Twenty Miles From a Match

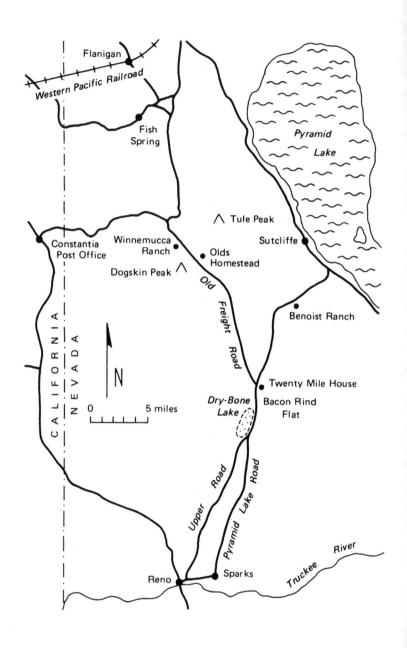

Twenty Miles From a Match

Homesteading in Western Nevada

Sarah E. Olds

Foreword by Leslie Zurfluh

UNIVERSITY OF NEVADA PRESS
Reno & Las Vegas

The descendants of Sarah Olds would like to thank Louis Beaupre,
Don Prusso, John Raker, and Kenneth Carpenter for their help
in bringing the present memoir to the attention of the
University of Nevada Press.

University of Nevada Press, Reno, Nevada 89557 USA
Copyright © 1978 by University of Nevada Press
All rights reserved
Printed in the United States of America
Book design by Dave Comstock

Library of Congress Cataloging-in-Publication Data
Olds, Sarah E., 1875–1963
Twenty miles from a match.
1. Olds, Sarah E. 1875–1963. 2. Washoe Co., Nev.—Biography.
3. Pioneers—Nevada—Washoe Co.—Biography. 4. Frontier
and pioneer life—Nevada—Washoe Co. I. Title.
F847.W3047   979.3'55'030924 [B]   78-13766
ISBN 0-87417-052-4

The paper used in this book meets the requirements of American
National Standard for Information Sciences—Permanence of Paper
for Printed Library Materials, ANSI/NISO Z39.48-1992 (R2002).
Binding materials were selected for strength and durability.

ISBN-13: 978-0-87417-052-8 (pbk. : alk. paper)

Contents

Foreword vii
Chapter One 1
  Two 13
  Three 20
  Four 30
  Five 37
  Six 47
  Seven 54
  Eight 62
  Nine 77
  Ten 85
  Eleven 94
  Twelve 102
  Thirteen 111
  Fourteen 124
  Fifteen 131
  Sixteen 137
  Seventeen 146
  Eighteen 152
  Nineteen 162
  Twenty 170
  Twenty-One 178
  Twenty-Two 181

Foreword

The buildings are gone now, burned in the brush fires of the 1970s, and the pastures of the homestead have been absorbed by the neighboring ranch. The driving spirit of the place had moved on before that, so it was just another deserted place by then. Sarah E. Olds had gone on to other interests and finally at 88 to her well-earned rest, having attained her goals of educating her six children without help from outside, and incidentally enjoying life immensely in the process.

Sarah Elizabeth Thompson was born in Iowa in 1875, the youngest daughter of a family of nine. Her father, Alexander Thompson, had migrated from Scotland to Canada, where he met and married Mary Anne Harper, a recent migrant from Ireland; they soon moved to Iowa, settling on a farm near Ottumwa. The Thompsons' large family was spread over many years, so by the time Sarah was a young lady her older brothers and sisters were out on their own. A brother, Dave, was attracted to the mining booms of the far west, and though he returned to Iowa, his stories of his adventures prodded several members of the family to move. An older sister, Nettie, committed the shameful act of divorcing her husband, and went west to avoid the criticism directed at herself and her family. Meanwhile, Sarah had studied dressmaking—the only acceptable occupation for young ladies in the Bible Belt at the time.

Late in the 1890s Sarah's parents became ill, and as the youngest daughter, she stayed home to care for them until their deaths. By 1897 Sarah was free and 21 years old. Sister Nettie, the disgraced one, was living in Modesto, California, so in spite of dire warnings by the family members still in Iowa, and the disappointment of several "neighbor boys," Sarah departed for California. Nettie had made her own way by cooking and housekeeping, so she knew the mining camps of the southern Mother Lode were excellent pickings for anyone who could cook or sew. Sarah therefore set out for Sonora, an active mining camp, riding in a rockaway stage. After investigating work possibilities in Sonora, she found the best prospects were in the smaller camps near Sonora— Jamestown, Columbia, Stent. She chose Stent, eight miles southwest of Sonora, where she met A. J. Olds, a prospector and miner.

Albert J. Olds—known as A.J.—was a member of a quite distinguished California family. His grandfather had come to Marin County in 1854 and bought 8,000 acres of land at Olema "for $4,000 gold coin." A.J.'s father had been a member of the Constitutional Convention for California, but A.J. and his brother were both bitten by the gold bug, and both drifted from one strike to another till their health failed. Today we know the disease as silicosis, but then it was the lethal "Miner's Con" that filled graveyards or wrecked health in camps from Bisbee to Virginia City. A record of the births of the Olds children is a record of the various mining discoveries of the period. Edson, the eldest, was born in Confidence, near Sonora,

California; Jessie in Bisbee, Arizona; Alice in Virginia City, Nevada. By then A.J.'s health had deteriorated so that he could no longer work underground, so the last three children, Leslie, Albert, and Martha, were born in Reno, where the family settled in 1906 (the last one after the homestead was established).

The homestead in 1910 must have been a discouraging sight. There were three rooms in a house of board-and-batten, with a shed roof. Sagebrush grew to the doorstep, and horses and cattle slept next to the house for lack of fences. There was a natural grass pasture, and much open range. The nearest neighboring ranches were owned by absentee ranchers and operated by hired hands, so our nearest family was twelve miles away, a Mexican family whose children were about the same age as Mom Olds's. All the children learned to ride at an early age, often bareback for want of a saddle, and usually on a mustang that could be had for the breaking.

The homestead was reached from Reno by following the Pyramid Lake road to the Twenty Mile House, then taking the old freight road which ran north toward Fish Springs and on into Oregon. Fifteen miles along this road is a small valley, containing two big ranches, and off to the east, the homestead. Tule Mountain rises east of the place, with wide natural meadows and springs in the high mountain, while Dogskin Mountain, steep and barren, looms to the west. A narrow, rocky canyon connects the valley to Warm Springs (now Palomino Valley) while to the north are two high passes over the mountains, usually snowed closed in winter.

By 1926 all the Olds children—or "homestead kids" as we were sometimes called—were away from the homestead, at school or married, so Sarah, by then known as Mom Olds to the ranchers and cowboys, launched on a new career. At Pyramid Lake was a fishing camp called Sutcliffe, or The Willows, one of the few privately deeded lands on the Paiute Reservation. The resort consisted of a motley array of tent houses and shacks, but was very popular with sportsmen. Maggie Sutcliffe had died, and her husband Uncle Jim had no way to operate the resort, so Mom Olds leased the property for a year and then bought it in 1927. She and A.J. were excellent hosts—Mom tending to the practical things, and A.J. entertaining guests with stories of the mines and early days. It was here that Mom wrote the bulk of her reminiscences about homesteading. Together they had the main building replaced and then the tents disappeared, so Sutcliffe became a thriving resort. The only hired help were Indian women for laundry and dishwashing, as the three younger children were home during vacations, the busiest time. We girls really worked those summers—but had fun too. Many times we would go to dances in Fernley or Flannigan—both about twenty miles away—and return just in time for a dip in the lake before serving breakfast to the fishermen.

In 1927 the state legislature changed Nevada's residency requirement (for divorce) from six months to three months, and divorcees from the Eastern states began crowding into Reno. There were only two main hotels then, the Golden and the Riverside, so the lawyers began placing clients out of town. Almost overnight several dude ranches started, and Sutcliffe became a dude ranch as well as a fishing resort. Other dude ranches near Pyramid were the Monte Cristo and the TH, followed by ranches in the Truckee Meadows and Franktown. Much to our disgust, we girls were delegated to take our "dudes" riding into the mountains—sometimes with hilarious results. One woman, on coming to a very steep place on a trail, declared in elegant Bostonian "I'm not going to ride down that Goddam precipice!" and it took an hour of persuasion to induce her to even walk down it, with us leading her horse ahead.

By 1928 A.J.'s health failed to the extent that he was bedfast most of the time, and one more daughter was married, leaving Mom less help in running the resort. In 1931 she sold it and moved to Reno, where A.J. died the same year.

By then Nevada was feeling the results of the Great Depression, so Mom Olds was able to buy part of the Waltz Ranch south of Reno, near what is now Virginia Lake. Here she planned to establish another dude ranch, but the "Winter of the Big Hungry" was upon her. The Wingfield Banks in Reno closed their doors, many businesses failed, and Mom's popularity became a debit, not an asset. The big Waltz house filled with unemployed cowboys and people out of work, rather than paying guests, and Mom hadn't the heart to refuse food and shelter. She leased the big house to a more hard-hearted couple, and built a small house across Lakeside Drive, where the Lakeside Plaza Shopping Center now stands. Here she lived most of the time, taking an occasional paying guest, traveling, and revising her reminiscences about life as a homesteader. Her travels took her to Alaska, Hawaii, Mexico, and, when she was 85, to Florida and New York. She remained alert and energetic to the end of her life in 1963. She was active in the Unity Church, and even went on national television to tell how she got her six children educated. The week before her death, she won a local cribbage tournament, and bridge was a constant interest.

Mom Olds' children did not fail her by accepting "outside help." Her efforts to educate them may have cost Nevada, but the cost was amply repaid over the years. The boys balked at college, but the four girls worked and got their Normal School certificates. Each taught school a year or two before marrying. From the 1920s to the start of World War II it was a crime for a female teacher to marry, so all stopped teaching and raised their families. Jessie was the first to return to teaching in rural schools, but by 1942 all four were back at work, and all finished University after the time out for families. In all, the Olds girls returned over 120 years of teaching for their initial cost of education. Edson, the trapper, continued in that line, with time out for service in the Seabees during World War II. He became an excellent judge of furs, and at the time of his death was affiliated with a large New York firm of furriers, the only Gentile in a company of Jewish businessmen. He was on a fur-buying trip in the hinterlands when he suffered a fatal heart attack at 72.

Albert was just out of high school when the Depression hit. He worked at various jobs in farming and mining, and finally found his niche as a gyppo logger in Quincy, California, where he now lives in very active retirement.

Alice was teaching in Henderson, Nevada, when she and her husband were killed in a head-on car crash. The other three girls are now retired, living in various parts of the state. Each produced from two to four children, all energetic, none on welfare—Mom's greatest dread. Not a bad record for a bunch of homesteaders' kids and a woman who started from scratch.

FERNLEY, NEVADA   LESLIE OLDS ZURFLUH
APRIL 1978

]| **One** |[

Biff, bang, bing went the snowballs against the side of my apartment at five A.M. We were having an unprecedented snow storm in the foothills of Tuolumne County, California. I was a young girl twenty-three years old, a tenderfoot or greenhorn, right out from Iowa. It was 1898, my first winter in California. I was operating a dressmaking shop in the little mining camp of Stent near Sonora. When the storm blew up the boys of the camp had promised me a good, old-fashioned face washing to remind me of home. They were true to their word, for here they were already throwing snowballs and threatening to break in if I didn't come out and play snowballs with them.

There were two girls living next door to me in a little home boarding house, the type of which there are always so many in any mining camp. They had promised to help me out in the fight. When they heard the fun begin, out they came. It was we three girls against a pack of rowdy boys. There were two inches of new, wet snow, which soon became mixed with red clay. What fun we had! We played and hollered till the snow melted and we all got wet, muddy, and tired.

The camp boasted of a few dug wells, our only water supply, one of which was next door to me in front of the boarding hose. After our snow battle I crossed over to the well for a bucket of water to clean myself and my apartment, which had been tracked with red clay inside and out. While I was drawing the water, a man came out of the boarding house rubbing his eyes, and hardly looking at me he said, "Why in hell don't you get down in the back yard or some back alley if you're going to yell around here like a pack of Piutes?"

As I was the only human in sight, his remarks were addressed to me. Thus were the first words spoken to me by the man who was to become my husband a few short months later. I had seen him going to and from the boarding house for months, and I knew his name was Mr. Olds, but until now we had never spoken.

I knew who he was, for he and I had helped substantially in supporting a lady and two children a few months before. Our charitable work came about in this way. Mr. Olds had a friend, a big Scotchman by the name of Herb McNeal, who was jovial when sober, but quarrelsome when drunk.

One night Herb got on a drinking spree, had a fight, and was shot twice through the hip. Mr. Olds hired a livery conveyance and with the help of another man got Herb to the hospital in Sonora, eight miles away. Next morning when he got home he went down to see how Mrs. McNeal and the two children were going to live while Herb was out of work.

He found them with no means of support. He had given her ten dollars with the promise of more when that was gone. This is where I came into the picture. A little boy came into the shop one day, stood looking straight at me for a moment, then exclaimed, "Miss Thompson, you have beautiful teeth."

I smiled and said, "Thank you, little fellow, thank
you. Whose little boy are you, and what is your
name?"

"I'm Bobby McNeal, and my daddy's in the hospital. I have a little cocker spaniel puppy with a long
tail. Daddy said we'd have to find somebody with
good teeth to bite the puppy's tail off. You have such
good teeth, won't you please come home with me
and bite off my puppy's tail?"

The little boy looked so earnest that I didn't dare
laugh at him. I knew he was the son of the man who
had been shot. "I would like to come home with you
and see your puppy, but I won't promise to bite off
his tail." I was curious to know what had prompted
such a queer request, and also anxious to see how
Mrs. McNeal was getting along without a payday, for
I knew miners well enough to know that one payday
barely reached the next.

Mrs. McNeal told me that her husband thought it
much better to bite a puppy's tail off than to cut it off,
and had jokingly remarked, "Miss Thompson, the
dressmaker, has such beautiful teeth we should ask
her to come down and do it." After Herb went to the
hospital, Bobby became the man of the family and
took it upon himself to see that the puppy's tail was
properly taken care of.

I found the family in need of help so told Mrs.
McNeal that I was a dressmaker and batching and
didn't have much time to cook. I suggested that I
would furnish the food for all of us for the evening
meal, if she would cook it. It would be a favor to me,
if I could come down and eat with them. In that way
Mr. Olds and I had kept the McNeal family for almost
two months until Herb was able to go back to work.

Although I had never met Mr. Olds, I had often

heard Mrs. McNeal tell what a wonderful man he was. At the time of our first encounter, he was trying to work nights at the mine and sleep in the daytime, and we in our hilarious fun had disturbed his rest.

"Oh, Mr. Olds," I said, "I'm very sorry we disturbed you."

"It's too late to be sorry now," he snapped. "There's no apologies accepted." He turned abruptly and went back into the house, leaving me thinking he was the darndest old crank I'd ever met.

I told everyone what I thought of him, wanting them to share in my opinion. Perhaps I was a little egotistical and stuck on myself, for I was used to hearing compliments rather than a tirade like this. The world in general had gone wrong with Mr. Olds that morning, and after his rude awakening he went down to the mine office, drew his time, and left town.

We didn't see him again for some time. I felt so bitter about him I really hoped he would never return. Not so with the boarding house girls. They said he was "awful good pay" and they hated to lose him.

In the meantime I was very much interested in a dashing young Irishman named Murphy, who was foreman of one of the mines. He had a wonderful baritone voice, and I realize now that it was the voice and not the man that I thought I was in love with. We were keeping steady company, as we called it in the gay nineties.

Mr. Murphy was very methodical in his courting. He called on me every Sunday and Wednesday evening promptly at seven P.M. Our chief enjoyment was going to concerts where he had engagements to sing. I would sit enraptured while listening to his melodious voice. The first song I heard him sing was "Esthore," meaning "darling" in Gaelic. I would imagine he was singing it to me. I still remember two lines that went like this:

> The waves are still singing to the shore,
> While I'm thinking of you, Esthore.

One afternoon while I was sitting on my porch sewing, I looked up and saw the most handsomely dressed gentleman walking my way. He wore a tailor-made suit and a derby hat, which was the fashion in those days. He stopped, tipped his hat, and said, "Good evening, Miss Thompson. I came over to apologize rather belatedly for my rudeness in speaking to you the way I did the morning of your snow battle."

It was then I recognized the well-dressed gentleman as Mr. Olds, the "old crank," the "detestable person" about whom I had made such unfavorable remarks. He was now a handsome young knight with a pleasant smile, and a very pleasing personality. But I could not resist the cutting remark, "It's too late to be sorry. No apologies accepted."

The apologies were accepted by both of us, for he came up on the porch and sat down for a friendly visit which lasted for hours. It was the beginning of a strange courtship that held never a word of love or affection, but a very real companionship. He called me either "Sister" or "old lady" from the beginning, which pleased me, for I thought it more interesting than the endearing terms the other young men used. I called him A.J. from the first, and so it was—A.J. and old lady (till we were married and the babies came, when he became Daddy to all of us).

A.J. liked to hunt and fish. He would come by my shop after coming off shift at the mine and say,

"Come on, old lady, let's take to the hills." I would neglect my work, and we would go for a glorious tramp, either hunting or fishing along the Tuolumne River.

One day while fishing, we found an old raft tied up to a stump. Some children had made it and anchored it there. It was rather a crude affair—just two big logs with boards nailed on top. We thought it would be fun to row the raft out in the middle of the river where the water was deep so A.J. could fly-cast from it.

It was great fun. A.J. finally caught his fish, but in the excitement of reeling it in he stepped too close to the edge of the raft, dumping both of us into the water. I had learned to swim bare-naked as a child, but we never knew what a bathing suit was. This was a different proposition. Swimming now in the swift-moving current with all my clothes on was quite a struggle. I was fully dressed in the costume of the gay nineties—high-topped button shoes, black lisle stockings, two full, ruffled petticoats, and an ankle-length dress. It was topped off with a wide-brimmed sailor hat fastened on with two ten-inch hatpins stuck in from opposite sides of the crown. It would have been an acrobatic feat to remove my hat. I laboriously swam in all my cumbersome attire through the fast-flowing stream. Fortunately I had only a few strokes to swim till I reached shallow water and waded ashore.

I think A.J. must have glanced my way and seen that I was making it all right, for he kept right on with his fish. Soon he followed me to shore with both fish and raft. After depositing his hard-won fish on the bank, he came over and gave me a rousing smack on my wet back and said, "By George, old lady, you're all right!"

We went on our hiking and fishing trips almost every evening except Wednesday and Sunday. These nights were still reserved for Mr. Murphy. A.J. insisted that I keep those dates. I was becoming very fond of A.J. and wished he would say some little word of love or ask me to discontinue seeing Murphy, but there was never a word, and when Murphy's name was mentioned A.J. had only the greatest praise for him.

One evening while A.J. was hurrying me home to keep my Wednesday night date I said boldly, "A.J., I have lots more fun with you than I do with him. I'll quit him if you'd like me to."

Much to the deflation of my ego A.J. replied, "No, old lady. Don't you do it! Never give up a good man for a poor one. Murphy has everything a young girl would want. He's a handsome fellow with a wonderful voice and social position. He's foreman of one of the biggest mines around here, and he must have money.

"Then look at me. Just a hobo miner. You might call me a ten-day man. I just stay on one job long enough to make a stake to move on to the next. I want to rove, to ramble, to venture, to see what the next turn in the road holds for me. Someday I'll strike it rich—then everything will be different."

That last remark expressed the hopes and dreams of every miner I ever knew. They are all an optimistic bunch. No matter what poverty or privation they may endure, someday they're all going to strike it rich.

"No, old lady," A.J. repeated, "you grab Murphy if you can. Someday you'll be rich."

On the other hand, Mr. Murphy's attitude toward

A.J. was so different. Some little bird had told him of A.J.'s calls, and our delightful companionship irked him. He had heard that A.J. gambled all his money, he told me, and he knew one payday never reached the next for him. "How can you tolerate such a bum?" he asked me. "Will you please tell him to take his companionable walks with someone else?"

Of course we quarreled, and I told him not to come to see me anymore. I was honestly glad of a chance to break our friendship, but when I told A.J. about it he seemed very sad. He said he was sorry that he had ever come into my life, but we still continued our rambles.

I had a sister living on a ranch five miles from Stent by wagon road, but it was only three miles by a beautiful mountain trail that led us across the Tuolumne River. We had to cross a foot bridge, which was suspended by cables fastened into the canyon walls, and it swung high above the turbulent waters. At that spot the canyon opened into a little valley with a view of a fruit ranch below. There my memory plays tricks on me, for the only memory I have retained of it is with the fruit trees in bloom, surrounding the weather-beaten old house that was literally covered with rambling roses. We would stand together on the swinging bridge, and I would exclaim in awe at the beauty of the scene below, "Beautiful, beautiful, beautiful!"

A.J. would look down at the same scene and say, "Who in hell would live there? It's isolated. The only place you can see is up."

"What difference does it make if it's in the heart of Egypt," I would retort, "if it's a home and a beautiful one." I think I was subconsciously longing for a home and wishing that little ranch was mine. We realized then for the first time what a difference of opinion we held on almost everything. A difference which we carried all through life. But I believed then, and still believe, that if there is enough love it can surmount any difficulty.

In a mining camp where there are so many men and so few women, a girl gets lots of attention and many proposals of marriage. But A.J. was so different from the rest. I will admit now that from his very first visit I was madly in love with him, and although I called him an "old crank" to everyone, I felt flattered and flustered whenever he appeared and turned on all the charm I could muster. But as far as love went, I could never induce him to say one word or make a move in my direction, or even say that he approved of me.

Then the roving spirit struck him and the hills were greener on the other side. He left for Bodie, a mining camp across the Sierra mountains, where miners' wages had reached the fabulous sum of four dollars a day. I tried to persuade him to stay in Stent, but to no avail.

The morning he left he came by my shop and bid a friendly good-bye, asking me to write to him. "Just Bodie, California," he said in reply to my request for his address. Then he added, "All girls seem to have a weakness for writing, so practice on me."

This made me think, "Well, you old crank, I bet I never do write to you."

How I missed him! I listened each evening for his decided and individual footsteps on the newly macadamized road that ran by my door. In my mind I was sure I could hear him coming. Then I would remind myself that if he didn't think enough of me to say one little word of love, it was a good thing for me that he was gone and I'd better forget about him. Then I'd add for my own satisfaction, "He was an awful old crank anyway."

A week or more had passed when I received a friendly little note from A.J. at his Bodie address. I didn't answer it. I was still hurt to think he hadn't even given me a good-bye kiss, and at the same time I was being entertained by a thriving, handsome young doctor, who had a beautiful horse and buggy in which he took me riding every evening. I was having a good time and was determined to forget A.J., whom I firmly believed didn't care a hoot about me.

Then I had another note from him saying that he had written to me but received no reply, and thought surely I had not received his letter. I didn't answer that one either.

Thought I, "Old boy, you'll have to declare some interest in me before I ever so much as write a line to you." I was making a good try at forgetting him by accepting the attention of the young doctor. I wondered then, and have many times since, why I couldn't have fallen in love with the doctor, who made a fuss over me and proposed marriage, and lavished all kinds of attention on me. He had a wonderful career ahead of him.

Instead I chose a broken-down old miner, sixteen years my senior. The only explanation I can give is that God directs love and we humans have very little to do with it. A.J. was still on my mind, and though I vowed not to write to him, I simply couldn't forget him.

Then another letter came, this time much more to my liking. Still there was no word of love, but why, he wanted to know, hadn't I written? I had given him reason to think, his letter said, that I cared a little more for him than I did for the other boys. He had thought I was one girl he could rely on, and that I wasn't just a flirt playing with some poor devil's heart.

Thought I, "I won't answer that either. If he really cares for me, he can come back to say so."

Imagine my great satisfaction when, about a week later, up on the hurricane deck of the incoming stage, I recognized the dust covered figure of A.J. Olds. I know that nothing but the eyes of love could have discerned through that crust of red dust and the coming of dark, the figure of the man they loved.

The doctor was sitting on the porch with me when the stage arrived. When I realized that it really was A.J. on top of the stage there never in all my life was such a moment of ecstasy. I forgot all about the doctor sitting there. I jumped up, and like a happy child I clapped my hands with joy and exclaimed, "Oh, there's A.J. Olds." I knew instinctively in that moment that he had come back to me, and for me.

The doctor arose, tipped his hat, and said, "Good-bye, Miss Thompson, I see the lay of the land, and if I ever call on you again it'll be professionally." Then he was gone.

I sat there in the dark waiting. I had waited only a few minutes when I heard the longed-for footsteps come to my gate. I went to meet him and would have thrown my arms around him, dust covered and dirty as he was, but he would not allow it. He caught me by the arms, and with he on one side of the low fence and I on the other, he delivered a tirade of accusations and abuse. "If a fellow really cared for a girl, and she gave him every reason to think she cared for him in return, and deliberately led him on just to have the glory of breaking one more heart, well, I think there should be a special name made for that kind of a girl, and you're it. And I'm guilty of being in love with you! While I knew you wouldn't care a damn, I just had to come back and tell you about it! So there! I have confessed. It was a sneaking regard for you that brought me back. Now you have another heart to hang on your charm-string."

Then he put his hand on my face, pressing gently and said, "Now, old lady, if you're going to marry me you've got to say so right now, and we'll get married and camp under a tree, for I haven't a damn cent. What d'ya say?"

I had been waiting all this time for the tirade to be over so I could say yes. Now I said it.

"Good God, old lady! Do you mean it?" And it didn't take him long to jump that low fence. He didn't even stop to open the gate. Then our arms went around each other in one long embrace.

⅜[**Two**]⅝

Not long after that A.J. came by one evening driving a horse and buggy he'd rented from a livery stable, and called out, "Come on, old lady. We're taking a buggy ride."

When we drove off he told me he'd borrowed twenty dollars, and we were going to Sonora to get married. We ran into a friend and took him along to help get the marriage license and witness the ceremony.

In our earlier acquaintance, A.J. had noticed that I had exceptionally large feet, owing I expect to going bare-foot as a child in the plowed field of our Iowa farm. I was always very sensitive about my big feet. A.J. noticed this and during almost every visit would manage to ask, "What size shoe do you wear?"

I had also learned he was very sensitive about his age, so when he would ask about the size of my shoe I would counter with, "How old are you?" It became a standing joke between us with neither of us knowing the answer.

The morning of the wedding when the preacher handed him the marriage certificate to sign, he wrote in his age. Then he passed the certificate on to me to sign. Curiosity or some compelling force caused me to look to see how old he was, and standing there before the preacher and the witnesses he nudged me with his elbow and said, "Now, old lady, what size shoe do you wear?" I was never so embarrassed in my life, but I was learning fast that my new husband had individual ways of his own. There never was anyone else like him.

Right after the ceremony as the four of us were walking down the street, we passed a grocery store that had the scales sitting on the sidewalk out in front.

A.J. said, "Old lady, let's get weighed and see who's boss. The biggest man wears the pants." He stepped on the scales and tipped them to 165 pounds. I tipped them at 168! I've been the boss ever since, but I don't think A.J. ever knew it.

Our marriage certificate was in book form with lovely wedding bells on it. The first of its kind that I had ever seen. Back in my home everyone had their marriage certificate framed and hanging on the parlor wall. Once or twice a year the parlor was opened and you could view the pictures along with the marriage certificate while sitting on the stiff black horsehair furniture. This new book certificate was much to my liking, for I could always keep it in my baggage and I knew it would be some time before I'd have a home to hang it in. I was going to cherish that little book, but alas! I never got it. The minister had us sign it and said he would take it to the court house and have it recorded, then send it to us in the mail.

In reading the early morning paper next day my husband suddenly exclaimed, "Good God, old lady! We've killed the preacher."

The minister had taken the certificate to the court house and had it recorded, and then dropped dead on the way home. We never got our certificate, but we found it was recorded in the court house in Sonora, where if ever needed we could get a record of it.

Then began a series of moves from one mining camp to another. We went from California to Oregon, to Arizona, to Nevada. These moves lasted for the next twelve years, for with all miners the hills are greener far away. The distance of our journey depended entirely on the size and fleshiness of our purse.

Our life reminded me so much of Charles Dickens's description of the Micawber family in his book *David Copperfield*. I also saw the movie and felt so sorry for Mrs. Micawber, who with each move and each new baby looked more worn, more pale and discouraged. Only in our case it was my husband who looked discouraged and toilworn, for our moves and our babies both came often.

Early in our married life my husband developed what is now known as silicosis. Then it was simply miner's consumption, or as the miners glibly called it, "miner's con." A.J., whom I now called Daddy, and a friend of his always joked about their miner's con and what nice-looking young widows they were going to leave. But with me it was no joke. I became discouraged seeing my poor tired husband looking for a job, which he knew in advance he had neither the health nor the strength to hold.

By this time we had five children and no money, but I had almost superhuman health and strength. I began looking for something where I could help make a living.

By 1907 we were living in Reno, Nevada, and had been for the past two years—our longest stay in any one place. Daddy had obtained a little one-horse transfer outfit, but his health had failed till he wasn't strong enough to do even that. We were living on the outskirts of Reno where we had two cows, one hundred and fifty chickens, and a big garden. I sold milk, eggs, and some garden stuff. Of course this all helped, but it wasn't enough to make a complete living. I wanted a ranch, and how badly I wanted it! Having been raised on a farm in Iowa, I felt instinctively that if I could only get on a ranch I could make a living for our little brood and give my dear A.J. a chance to rest.

The doctor had told me two years before that only rest, fresh air, and sunshine would ever do him any good, for he was beyond human help. With no money how was I going to get my ranch? I kept looking and kept faith that something would turn up. Something did in a most unexpected way.

Daddy's nephew by marriage, Hiram West, a young cowboy, had homesteaded out on Tule Mountain, thirty-five miles north of Reno. There were droves of wild horses roving over the Nevada hills. That was before the government hired men to go out and rid the range of wild horses, which the ranchers claimed depleted the range of grass; and even worse, when they turned their blooded brood mares out, they said, the mares always bred to wild stallions instead of to blooded stock, making their offspring almost worthless.

Hi's only means of support was to break the wild horses, gentle them, and sell them in Reno. He had about five acres of grass fenced around his cabin, and a big stockade corral built to hold a group of wild horses.

In talking to Hi one day he told me of a piece of

vacant land adjoining his on the south, which interested me very much. But how was I going to get Daddy, who was never a rancher, to homestead? That was quite a problem. But again something told me to have faith, and if it was the right thing to do, a way would open up.

In talking to Daddy about ranches he always expressed as his opinion, "A ranch is a place where you have to work sixteen hours a day and wear patched overalls."

I thought a ranch was a place where one could make a living in God's fresh air and sunshine. Again, our difference of opinion.

My friends were all advising me to apply to the county for help. They said with an invalid husband and all those little children, the county would readily help us. That idea didn't appeal to me. There was no organized relief at that time, for which I am thankful to this day, for if there had been, I might have accepted help, and I have always had a horror of being an object of charity.

After my homesteading talk with Hi, I didn't let the idea get out of my mind. He told me Tule Mountain was the greatest game country ever laid out of doors. There were droves of deer, literally thousands of sage hen, coveys of mountain and valley quail, and doves galore, some cottontail, and of course the much despised old jack rabbit. All this added fuel to the homesteading scheme which was fast developing in my mind. My biggest problem was in getting A.J. interested enough to file papers on a homestead. I could just hear him saying, "Why, old lady, you're crazy. It simply can't be done!"

However, my idea persisted and my thoughts were

steadily forming. Daddy was quite a sportsman and liked to hunt and fish when he was able. That was my trading point. I now planned a hunting trip with Hi. He was to get Daddy to go hunting with him on Tule Mountain. The plan worked like a charm. Daddy went hunting with Hi, and came home so enthused with his success. Why, he could shoot sage hen right out of Hi's front door, and he went on to tell me about all the other game that abounded out there.

Hi wanted a neighbor and was almost as enthusiastic about my homesteading plan as I was. He told Daddy of some land open to homesteading, and stressed the abundance of game and the good trout fishing in nearby Pyramid Lake. By the time they returned from their hunting trip Daddy was all pepped up to go out there and homestead. I didn't let any grass grow under my feet in encouraging him to go to Carson City and file the papers.

I had triumphed easily over my first stumbling block. Never had a scheme worked so smoothly. It was the greatest piece of strategy I ever managed, and Daddy never realized it.

All that fall and winter we made great plans for the homestead in the following spring. Daddy said he would build a cabin, a kind of hunting lodge where he could go in the summer to rest, hunt, and fish when he was able, but he didn't include me in any of his homestead plans. I was to stay in Reno and run our chicken ranch, small as it was, and the dairy route from our two cows. I readily agreed to all his plans, but insisted that the cabin must have two rooms in it. One bright spring morning, Daddy, with another old broken-down miner, whom we always seemed to help support from our meager income, borrowed a team and wagon, and bought enough lumber to build the cabin. Away they went on their first venture at carpentry. I had drawn the plans for the cabin, confidentially knowing I would soon occupy it. It was to have two good-sized rooms, twelve by fourteen, with a small extension on the back, six by eight, for a pantry and clothes closet.

During the winter I had managed to lay away one hundred and fifty dollars, which was to build the cabin and pay to move us out there. Not until they returned from building the house did I announce that I was going homesteading too.

Great was Daddy's consternation and many were his objections. "Why, you're crazy, old lady! It can't be done! What in hell could you do out there with a bunch of little kids?"

I came back with, "What could you do out there without me?"

He was searching his mind for objections, anything that would keep me from going out there. He finally hit upon a good one. An idea that almost wrecked my plans and really looked insurmountable. "You simply can't take five little kids thirty-five miles from a school!"

That stumped me. I knew it was all too true.

引 Three 后

I was entirely ignorant of school law or how one went about organizing a school district, but I made up my mind to find out. I never for an instant let up on my plans, only enlarged them. Each hindrance only seemed to strengthen my determination to surmount all obstacles. I learned the county commissioners were the ones to establish a new school district. One of our Reno neighbors, Ed Ferris, was a county commissioner. I lost no time in seeing him and told him of our homestead plans. I asked what the chances were of organizing a school where there were no other children but our five. Ed was a big jovial fellow. He gave a hearty laugh, slapping me on the shoulder with a, "Ha, ha! Mrs. Olds, you have kids enough of your own to move out in the sagebrush anyplace and demand that the state erect and support a school for you. It only requires five children to organize a school district in Nevada."

What wonderful words. I was simply jubilant. My dreams were coming true. I knew Daddy was still staunchly objecting, but things had worked out my way. My good news put faith in my heart and wings to my feet.

We were two miles from Ed Ferris's place by wagon road, but not nearly so far across the fields. Going home, I skipped across fields, jumped irrigation ditches, crawled through barbed wire fences, and burst into our house tired and breathless. I threw my arms around Daddy's neck and announced my good news. Then giving him a big hug I said, "So now, what's keeping us? Let's go homesteading!"

"All right, old lady. Do as you damn please. You will anyway!" I knew when he said that, that he had decided I was right. That was just Daddy's masculine way of surrender. Once he did surrender he would always join in my proposition so wholeheartedly that one would think it was all his idea in the first place.

From then on we planned together on what we would do and how to make money to live on, for we had to start from scratch. There were no game laws in Nevada at that time, so our plans of survival were these. Daddy would kill game, each in its own natural season, and I would take it to Reno and sell it.

What great plans we made while lying awake nights! How strange that in making plans one never includes the difficulties they may encounter. We never once thought about washouts, droughts, or sickness. Owing to Daddy's health I should have included sickness, but I didn't. I was so sure that with rest, fresh air, and sunshine, Daddy would recover. That was the only real disappointment we ever had on the homestead. He partially recovered and God left him with us for the next twenty years, but he was never strong again, or able to do much manual labor.

Apparently I thrived on hard work. I think there was never a woman blessed with better health than I. I seemed to have strength enough for both of us.

Our move to the homestead was of great concern to all our neighbors, friends, and relatives. They all predicted hardships and starvation, and said, "It can't be done."

One old neighbor came the morning we left with a little bunch of fruit trees and some gooseberry and currant bushes and cuttings in his wagon. He gave me the only friendly advice and encouragement that I had heard from anyone. "Mrs. Olds," he told me, "I know with your youth and strength you can do it."

We had hired two teamsters to haul our furniture and supplies out to the homestead. The neighbors were all there with tears and dire predictions to bid us good-bye. With their sad farewells in my ears I said, "Don't say good-bye to me. You're the nearest neighbors I have, and I'm not going to say good-bye to you every time I see you." I waved to them, picked up the lines, and started out singing "Sweet Betsy From Pike"—although I think "sweet Betsy" had more worldly goods when she started over the mountains than we had when we started homesteading. We must have made a queer looking procession going through town. Our start in ranching consisted of two milk cows, a yearling Jersey heifer, a three-day-old calf, a tall, bony old gray horse named Johnny, and a spring wagon.

The three little girls, Jessie, Alice, and Leslie, and myself were perched up on the seat of the wagon. I held the fifteen-month-old baby, Albert, on my lap, and held the calf firmly between my feet while driving the old horse. Altogether it was a strained way to ride thirty-five miles. Our oldest son, Edson, was sitting in the back of the wagon on top of the chicken brooder, which held fifty baby chicks. He held the lead ropes of the two milk cows. Daddy, walking behind with the buggy whip, tapped them with the whip to keep them in pace with the horse and herded the yearling heifer, which was loose. These were city cows and like ourselves were headed for an entirely new way of life.

Our trip through town was slow. Dogs ran out to bark, scaring the cows and causing all kinds of delay. But when we reached the outskirts of town and started for the great open spaces we made better progress, and Daddy climbed into the wagon and up on the brooder with Edson.

Our first stop at the Eight Mile Spring was, as indicated, eight miles from Reno. We halted there for lunch. I had prepared enough food in a big grub box for the nine of us for two days. The teamsters had made better time than we and had a camp fire going and water boiling for coffee when we arrived. We unloaded the children and the calf, allowing them to play while we rested. Then we all ate. It had taken us five hours to make the first eight miles.

We had to make the Twenty Mile House that night, for that was the next water hole safe for drinking. True, there was Dry-Bone Lake a few miles ahead, but it was just one of those alkali slicks which abound in Nevada, a depression in the ground that fills each spring with the runoff from the melting snow in the hills. That spring there had been a big runoff, and Dry-Bone Lake was quite a body of water. It was at least three miles long and two miles wide, but only two feet deep. It was a terrible death trap for weak cattle turned out in the spring. The bottom of the lake was alkaline and sticky. The weak stock would wade in there to drink, get stuck, fall, struggle, and die. In a year or two, their dry bones would be shining on the shore—hence the name.

After lunching and resting, we plodded slowly along till about half a mile past Dry-Bone we started upgrade. Old Daisy, one of the old milk cows, lay down to rest. After letting her rest for half an hour of our precious time, we decided we'd have to get moving if we were to reach the Twenty Mile House before dark. We began trying to make her get up. We twisted her tail, hit her with the buggy whip (but not hard enough to have any effect), and Daddy cussed her, but old Daisy just lay there chewing her cud.

Finally after what seemed an age of delay, we had a happy thought. Maybe she needed a drink. We sent Edson back to Dry-Bone for a bucket of water. He didn't have much water left in his open bucket after a half-mile walk, but it was enough, for Daisy would have none of it. This made Daddy so furious that he grabbed the pail, throwing the water in her face with the ejaculation, "There, you damned old bitch! Take that!" It had the desired effect. It scared Daisy and she jumped up. Our present troubles were over, and we anxiously started on, for the sun was getting low and we had several miles to go.

The children had heard us speak of the Twenty Mile House and thought of it as some great goal to be reached. They had been asking questions about it for hours. "When will we get there? What kind of beds will we have to sleep in?" and so on and on. The Twenty Mile House had, in former days, been a stopping place for big teams on the old Oregon trail. The big barn was still standing, but the original house had burned down, and there was only a three-room cabin in its place. It stood at the crossroads, one road going to Pyramid Lake, the other running northwest toward Surprise Valley in California.

Most of the time the house was uninhabited. Occasionally some old bachelor would move in. Laying in a good supply of liquor, he would sell water and give away the liquor, thus eliminating the problem of having to buy a liquor license. When the Twenty Mile House was open a man could always liquor up cheap. It was now supposed to be vacant. It had a good stove in it, and there was a plentiful supply of water.

We arrived just at dusk, and as we came around the bend in the road we could see the old barn and corrals. When the children, who had been stretching their necks in eagerness, saw the little weather-beaten board house, they were greatly discouraged. But look! There was friendly smoke coming out of the chimney, and someone was ringing the old triangle supper iron.

We all unloaded and found the house occupied by the county road workers—ten men and a cook. The cook was a generous, good-natured fellow, for when he saw us drive in, he hollered, "Come and get it!"

We hesitated. There were nine of us. But the cook insisted we come in and eat. There was plenty for all, he said.

What a meal—a great platter of ham and eggs, stacks of hot biscuits, boiled potatoes with the jackets on, and bowls of brown gravy. For dessert there was the inevitable bowl of stewed dried peaches. You will always find dried fruit of some variety in any desert or cow camp, and if cooked properly it is surprising how tasty it is.

The road crew had built bunks in the house and put straw in them for mattresses, which they now vacated in honor of us, and went to the barn with their bedding.

We bedded down in their bunks. The next morning the children came running to me exclaiming, "Oh,

Mama, will we have such nice beds as that on the homestead?'' The long, tiresome ride of the day before had fitted them for a good night's sleep in almost any kind of a bed.

We arose early with another good hot meal awaiting us. It was a duplicate of the night before. Those two hot meals were the only help I ever had from the county. We started early on the last lap of our journey to the homestead. It was a bright, beautiful morning in April, with the sun shining, the birds singing, and the spring desert flowers blooming.

In Nevada we have a little pink flower we call the sand flower. It grows out of the desert with its foliage flat on the ground almost covered with sand, leaving the pink bloom sticking straight up on an inch and a half stem. It grows in great clusters after a wet winter. On that lovely morning the desert was covered for miles and miles with a carpet of pink, and the bluebirds in great flocks were flitting back and forth across the road, and the beautiful painted hills off to our right were outstanding in all their rainbow hues. All Nature seemed to be giving us a welcome to our new home.

We stopped for lunch this second day in a canyon where there was a grassy spot below a bubbling spring. Every stop on our way to the homestead holds a place in my memory like a milepost on my road of life. We rested there awhile. The children were all tired and getting fussy, constantly asking, ''When do we get there? How much farther is it?'' Only the little four-year-old Leslie was happy and contented. When we would ask her how she was getting along she would answer with the brightest smile, ''Pitty fine!'' It was such an inspiration to hear that little "Pitty fine!" that we asked it often just to bolster up our own morale.

There were five more weary miles to go.

Our homestead was inside a big company field. In the old days a company would fence miles of land they had no title to. Such a one was the PF company. Our property was all inside their fence and a mile from the main road. As we passed through the meadow the grass was up to the hubs of our wagon wheels.

We arrived at the cabin about four P.M. Daddy had gone on with the teamsters from our lunch stop and was at the cabin to greet us when we arrived. He held up his arms to give me a lift out of the wagon. I put one foot on the step of the dashboard, reached to Daddy's helping hand and jumped, and with more luck than skill my skirts missed the brakes and wheels, and I landed safely.

Daddy took me by the arm, led me to the cabin door, and with a grand sweep of his hand said, "There, old lady. There's your home, and it's damn near in the heart of Egypt." I'll admit it wasn't as beautiful as the little fruit ranch of long ago, but it looked good to me, and I was sure we could soon make it beautiful. It didn't look very good to our eight-year-old Jessie. When she saw the unfinished cabin she began to cry and said, "Is this the kind of an old place you brought us to?" True, the windows were not yet installed, and they had purposely left the door casings unfinished, for I had an old Home Comfort steel range that wouldn't go through an ordinary door. The carpenter's work bench was still in the kitchen, and the floor was covered with shavings.

"Yes, Jessie, this is our home, and everyone is

going to help make it look nice." At that she grabbed the broom and made the shavings fly.

The first glimpse I had of the home might have been discouraging to most people. There was the unfinished two-room cabin, our furniture sitting around in the sagebrush where the teamsters had unloaded it; I had a semi-invalid husband, and five little children aged from eleven years down to a fifteen-month-old baby, and one dollar and fifty cents left after paying the teamsters. No wonder my friends and relatives all said I was crazy. As I look back now, I think they put it mildly. But I was neither dismayed nor discouraged. There was never a general going into battle with more assurance of victory than I had of making a success of the homestead and of getting an education for the children.

One of the teamsters was a lanky fellow, very slow of speech. He had been raised out in the hills. Just in the way of conversation I said, "Well, what do you think of the layout?" When he hesitated, I quickly added, "Never mind answering that." I had heard so many detrimental remarks about our endeavor that I had insulated myself by not listening to what anyone had to say.

He drawled out, "Well, naow, I've seen a durn sight worse lookin' places than this." It wasn't exactly an encouraging remark, but it wasn't discouraging either.

There we were at last, planted on the homestead, with so many things to do, it was hard to decide what to do first. Since it was already late afternoon, the first business was preparing for the night. Jessie had done a good job clearing away the shavings. We moved the cookstove in and set it up. Then we finished the door casings and hung both doors.

There were a front door and a back door directly opposite each other, which proved to be a godsend till our trees grew big enough to furnish shade. The draft through the open doors was a blessing.

Our furnishings were meager. We set up the beds, brought in the table and chairs, and we were all ready for housekeeping.

We had a folding couch in the kitchen where Edson slept, and where later many another passerby joined him for a night's rest, for our little home, though a mile off the main road, soon became a stopping place for all who passed by.

Supper was simple that first evening. We were all too tired either to cook or eat. After a good night's rest we all felt fine and started in to make a success of the homestead.

We had always lived near a store where we could replenish the food as it disappeared. Now we were thirty-five miles from supplies. I had never known what it was to make a note of things as they gave out. Before we embarked on our homestead trip, I had bought what I considered enough food to last for months. Now I was surprised to see my "mountain" of food vanish in a very short time. One of our first problems was to work things out so as not to make any unnecessary trips to town.

We had been in our home about a week when this and that began to get scarce. Our one dollar and fifty cents began to look mighty small. It was then we thought of the three older children's banks. They each had a ten cent bank full making a total of thirty dollars. I had laid them away in the bottom of an old trunk and forgotten them. Now we were forced to break them open and use the money to buy grub.

⅜[**Four**]⅜

We had planned to go in as soon as possible to get our school organized. Now, needing grub, we could make one trip count double. Accordingly, Daddy hitched up Johnny and went to town to demand that the state organize a school district and build a school for us. What a disappointment he met.

I think it's human nature to believe what one wants to believe. When Mr. Ferris had told me, "You have children enough to move into the sagebrush anyplace and demand that the state erect a school for you," I believed it because I wanted to believe it. I was gloriously happy in believing it, so I never questioned his word or looked into the matter further, and I'm glad I didn't, for if I had, we never would have homesteaded. But here we were, all moved and settled, and it was rather late to learn we couldn't get a school.

When Daddy went to see the commissioners he was met with, "Oh, I'm afraid there's been a big mistake. You were certainly misinformed. It requires seven children to organize a new district—five of school age, and three in regular, daily attendance."

Daddy took their information as final, bought the groceries, and drove home, the most depressed and dejected person I have ever seen. Now that the trouble of moving was over, and with my optimism and encouragement, he had begun to think that if we got a school we could stay and our homestead would be a success. Now his hopes were dashed to the ground. Without a school it would be impossible to stay. Depressed as he was, however, the dear old boy was more worried about my disappointment than he was concerned with his own.

He came in, putting his arms around me and said, "Old lady, we're licked. We can't get a school. It's through no fault of our own, but we're licked. We'll just have to call it a nice summer's vacation, and when fall comes we'll pack our little doll rags and go back to town."

"But, Daddy, we can't go back. We've nothing to go back to, and nothing to go back on." We've all heard about the man who had a bear by the tail and couldn't let go. Well, that was us. Besides I wasn't licked. Call it faith, call it intuition, or just plain cussed stubbornness—maybe that's what it was, but whatever it was I had it. I never for one moment thought I wasn't going to get a school.

I know very well, that if the shoe had been on the other foot, so to speak, if it had been some project of Daddy's that had failed, especially one I had not been in favor of, I could not have resisted one little dig, one "I told you so!" But not so with Daddy. He was so concerned with my disappointment.

I thought there had been some mistake. Surely A.J. could have been more forceful in presenting his case. Something would turn up. There must be, there would be some way out.

I was racking my brain trying to think. We had five children now. If we just had two more that would be

it. Then I realized that by the time the two next
unborn babies were old enough to go to school, the
two older ones would be too old to draw rural school
money. I had to abandon that plan—it wouldn't
work. I'd never be able to have babies fast enough to
catch up to that school district! I still would not accept
defeat.

Accordingly, I made plans for a trip to Reno the
following week, after Johnny had a rest. On the next
Monday I put up a lunch to eat at the Twenty Mile
House. We made it a must to stop there and have a
cup of hot coffee. The thirty-five-mile trip always
required at least ten hours of slow, steady driving. A
hot lunch on the way was a wonderful pickup for the
hot trip. I had baked bread and left everything in
readiness for Daddy and the children while I would
be gone the three days. It always took one day to
drive in, one day to shop and transact any business,
and one day to drive home.

Now I was ready. My lunch in a bag, I had climbed
into the wagon and picked up the lines, when Daddy,
who had all the while protested what he called a
useless trip, came out. Leaning his foot on the hub of
the wagon wheel, he looked up at me and said, "Old
lady, that's a long hard trip to town, and what in hell
do you think you can accomplish that I haven't already done?"

"I don't know, Daddy. I only know we've got to
have a school, and I'm bettin' we get one." I hit old
Johnny a crack and moved on, happy in the thought
that some way we would have a school.

I drove slowly along the sandy road and after five
hours arrived at the Twenty Mile House. There was
no county crew here now. I went in, started a fire,

and made a cup of tea. The old place smelled of wood rats, as most vacant places in the hills do, so I went out on the doorstep to eat my lunch. Just then a fellow with a four-horse team and wagon drove up and stopped at the well to water his horses.

I called out, "Hi, Mister. Come and have lunch with me." He was a stranger that I had never seen before. Many people have asked, "Weren't you afraid to speak to a stranger way out there on the desert twenty miles from another human being?" I'm glad to say I wasn't. That kind of fear was left out of my makeup. It was a cheery invitation I called out to him to join me, and he came.

I filled up the tea cup I had brought along, handed it to him with one of the sandwiches I had packed, and we settled down to eat. I drank out of the tea can.

Doctors would call our ensuing conversation "case history." To us it was desert gossip and information. We asked each other's names, where we lived, and our occupations. He was a teamster hauling freight and an old-timer out there. In fact, he had been born out there. I told him where we were homesteading and my problem about a school, and that I was on my way to see the county commissioners to try and find a way to establish a school.

In his drawling voice he said, "Now, ain't that a piece a good luck. My Mother over there at the Pyramid school district has just been notified that she'll lose her school if more children don't come into her district by September first. She has only two children left of school age. If you'll join districts with her, you can divide the fund which is a thousand dollars a year, and then each of you can hold five months school. Mother expects to sell out this coming

summer, and if you can get the school organized
before she sells, you'll fall heir to the whole school
fund. Just go on in and have the commissioners ex-
tend the district lines to include your homestead."
That would be a twenty-mile stretch. Could I get
them to do it?

The rest of the long trip fled like magic. I was here,
then presto, I was there. I was so filled with wonderful emotions I never noticed that long hard trip.

The commissioners were meeting that evening,
and I was there to present my case. But to my great
concern, I met disappointment at every turn. The
head spokesman threw up his hands and said, "Moving district lines is out of our jurisdiction. We have
nothing to do with it. Go see old Charlie Stoddard in
the court house." I couldn't see him till the next
morning. Of course, I was up early next day parading
up and down waiting for the doors of the court house
to open. Mr. Stoddard, who was county recorder,
only repeated the same thing. "I have nothing at all to
do with it. Go see old Bill Fogg."

Mr. Fogg was our county clerk way down at the
other end of the business district, with an office in the
post office on Commercial Row. When I saw him the
same performance was repeated, only more so. He
was a slim, elderly fellow who had lost his voice,
making it impossible for him to speak above a
whisper; but he could pound good and loud on his
desk, which he did. He now said with all the strength
and vehemence he could muster, "I'll have nothing to
do with it! That Pyramid school district has been
moved around the desert from one rock to another
after that old woman for the last twenty years at a
great expense to the county. I'll have nothing to do

with it!'' He turned and walked away. But after taking a few steps he turned again, and shouted as nearly as he could, ''Go see old man Bray.'' Mr. Bray, I learned, was our school superintendent and lived at the north end of town ten blocks away. I was afoot, and had done all this running around on my own power, which was beginning to weaken a little. But my faith was still intact. This Mr. Bray might be a little more favorable toward my project. It was with hope and a little prayer that I knocked on his door. Mr. Bray answered my knock. I introduced myself and stated my business, telling him of my visits to different people, and how each one had passed the buck, so to speak.

''The commissioners said, 'Go see old Charlie Stoddard,' '' I explained. ''Old Charlie Stoddard said, 'Go see old Bill Fogg.' Old Bill Fogg said, 'Go see old man Bray.' Will you please tell me, are you the old man Bray I want to see?''

By this time we were both laughing. ''Yes, I think I am. Come in and we'll talk it over. I'm your school superintendent, and I sent Mrs. Benoist the notice that her school at Pyramid Lake would be closed this fall. We'll see what can be done.'' I was jubilant. This was the first word of encouragement I had heard since the day before when talking to the teamster. I told him of our plans. We had five children, I added, three of school age. He already knew of Mrs. Benoist's two. That made the seven needed for a district. Could we be allowed to stretch the district lines twenty miles? I told him Mrs. Benoist was considering selling out. If we could get the district established before she sold, we would fall heir to the whole school fund. He listened attentively, then pointed out that there was a little technical point there—that of stretching the lines twenty miles. The reason they had all passed the buck on to the next was that none of them had wanted to accept that responsibility. Mr. Fogg had been right, for the old lady had cost the county a lot of money for surveying each time she took a notion to move. But as she always had enough children of her own, she had been able to demand a school, and there was nothing they could do but survey a new district and move the old schoolhouse to a new location. This time she had run out of children, and she was requesting a favor which they were reluctant to grant. This, however, was different. I was a newcomer with a brood of children that needed an education. After some careful thought, Mr. Bray said, "We'll just declare the Pyramid school lines extended to take in the Olds homestead. We needn't put the county to the expense of surveying it. I will appoint you the district clerk, Mrs. Benoist the president, and I will be the third trustee and sign all the school warrants. You'll have to erect your own building, for the state can only pay the teacher's salary. We'll spend half the fund on your side of the mountain, and half on Mrs. Benoist's." So, there. That easily we had our school. I believe God had opened the way.

I was so anxious to get home with my news that I could scarcely contain myself, but old Johnny needed a rest after the long ride, and I had another errand.

 Five

Aneighbor lady had kindly set eight turkey eggs for me which were now hatched out. Next morning with my little turkeys tucked under my arm, I walked down to the livery stable, got my horse and wagon, and started home.

One of our sudden spring storms blew up, and although it was the eighth of May it was one of the coldest trips I ever made across the desert. My little turkeys were protected under the wagon canvas, but I was sitting out in the rain and snow wearing only a light spring coat. It rained, it snowed, and it sleeted while the wind blew a perfect gale. I finally had to get out and walk on the sheltered side of old Johnny to keep warm. I would walk till I was tired, then climb back into the wagon and sit till I'd nearly freeze. I think I walked nearly half of that thirty-five miles, but I was so happy over my good news that I didn't mind the discomfort.

When I got home, I burst into the house and hollered, "We got our school! We got our school!" Daddy was as jubilant over it as I.

I let old Johnny rest for a few days, then hitched him to the wagon and with the three little girls drove the twenty miles over to Mrs. Benoist's to get acquainted and tell her of our good news. I thought perhaps I could get some information about running school. I found her to be a woman in her early sixties. Her two remaining school age children were a girl of sixteen and a boy of seventeen, both in the eighth grade. They were brilliant children but had purposely held back in their work so as to hold the school. Holding the school was more of a financial asset than an educational one. The teacher's board was a financial aid, too, as Mrs. Benoist charged forty dollars a month.

In meeting Mrs. Benoist, I was both surprised and concerned about her appearance. Her hair, which had been brick red, was mixed with gray making it a real taffy color. Her beautiful blue eyes looked out of deep-set sockets in the most bony, wrinkled face I have ever seen. She gave one the feeling that she had recently been rescued from a famine district.

The wrinkled face made such an impression on my four-year-old Leslie that she climbed up on my lap and whispered, "Mama, what makes the lady's face so curly?"

Mrs. Benoist had been a widow for years, but her eighty-year-old mother-in-law still lived with her. During the day, she and the old lady got into an argument over something that had happened years before. The discussion became quite heated until the younger woman became a little ashamed of herself. Backing off into the kitchen just before she slammed the door, she said, "Mother, we won't argue any more about it, but I know I'm right!" Bang! went the kitchen door.

The old lady tossed her head and looking at me said, "What in hell does Liz know about it? She's a Johnny-come-lately in these parts. She's only been here fifty years."

I have now lived in Washoe County, Nevada, fifty-five years and like to think of myself as an old-timer, but by Grandma Benoist's standards I am still a Johnny-come-lately.

Arriving home that evening, I told Daddy of the wrinkles that the toil, care, and hardships of the desert had worn in Mrs. Benoist's face. If I thought that would happen to me, I told him, I'd be leaving the country at the first sign of a wrinkle.

True to our school agreement, Mrs. Benoist held five months of school on her side of Tule Mountain, and we held five months on our side. Eventually Mrs. Benoist sold out and moved away, and we fell heir to the whole school, which we held in our house for fourteen years. It cost the state of Nevada fourteen thousand dollars to put our six children through the eighth grade—a record topped only by Mrs. Benoist herself.

Now with the school established, we had to decide what to do next. First things must come first. We were so enthusiastic over the school, we would have liked to pitch in and erect the school building right away. Common sense told us that wouldn't come first. We had a whole year in which to hold this five months of school, so there was no immediate need for a building.

Our vegetable garden was our first need. Everything was painfully slow, for we had no plow, harrow, or scraper, and only one old horse. We had to work by hand with spade, shovel, mattock, pick, and hand rake.

Since A.J. was a miner, his greatest knowledge and contribution to the place was in developing water. He went to work digging and developing to bring three small springs together, which made a good spring of water to irrigate with. Then with pick, shovel, spade, and wheelbarrow he laboriously dug a small reservoir. The springs and reservoir were both on high ground, and underneath were acres of good virgin sagebrush land. While Daddy was employed developing water, the children and I cleared the sagebrush off a space of ground about one hundred feet square. Then Edson and I with mattock and spade turned over the ground for our new garden. It was slow work, but what a happy time we all had working together there in the sunshine. Even the baby was there, for the garden was a quarter of a mile from the cabin and none of the children could be left behind. When our garden was all planted we turned our attention to well digging.

Until now we had been hauling water clear from the garden reservoir. We dug our well just a few feet in back of the house, and we were able to strike water at a shallow depth. A.J. hit water at six feet, and at nine feet the flow was too strong to allow him to dig anymore.

We walled the well up with rocks within two feet of the surface of the ground. There we built a wide shelf all around the inside, and then finished walling the well to the surface.

The shelf was a godsend. It was our only refrigerator for years. Cream, butter, left-overs from the table—everything that needed cooling went into the well on that shelf.

Of course, we had to fence our garden with woven wire to keep out the jackrabbits, which necessitated a trip to town to buy wire. What were we going to use for money with which to buy the wire, I wondered.

We had an early spring and the sage hens had hatched early and were now big enough to eat. I suggested that instead of going in debt for the wire, Daddy should kill a couple dozen birds, and I should take them to Reno to sell them. At first he objected, "How do you know you can sell them?"

"Well, there are ten thousand people living in Reno, and out of that number, I'll bet there are two dozen who'll be willing to buy sage hens. It'll be my job to find that two dozen." That was the beginning of a new venture. What a wonderful thing it is to have confidence in one's self. I never for a moment doubted my ability to sell those birds. It was many years before I realized I had any sales ability. Later I was to remark boastfully, "I've sold everything from our ranch from a quart of gooseberries to a wagon-load of manure."

Daddy killed the sage hens, and I went to town with them. I had no trouble in selling them for a dollar apiece. I had chosen for my customers doctors, lawyers, and business men. No going around to back doors for me in order to sell my produce. I always dealt with men, for I found them not only willing but eager to buy my game. Right there I had established a business. If we could supply the game, we could always eat. We would never have to worry again where our next bill of grub was coming from. I sold my birds, bought some grub and the garden wire, and proudly returned home to fence the garden.

In making our homestead plans we had some friendly advice. One neighbor said, "Don't ever kill gopher snakes. You just can't raise a garden without 'em. They kill gophers and ground squirrels." We learned to distinguish the difference between a

gopher snake and a rattler. Although their markings
are much the same, the rattler is much brighter in
coloring, and has a more beautiful, slender body
with, of course, the string of rattles at the end of his
tail. Legend has it that a rattler grows one rattle for
each year. I don't know how true that is, but a snake
is likely to lose some of his rattles in crawling through
our sharp Nevada rocks and sagebrush.

We vowed not to kill gopher snakes. One day a
distant neighbor lady was down helping me tack a
quilt. We hadn't yet hung up the screens at the front
and back kitchen doors. Our quilt was laid across our
long, homemade pine table, and we were busily
working away, when in crawled a whalin' big gopher
snake. I screamed. There's simply something repul-
sive and uncanny looking about a snake. I didn't
want to hurt it, so I got the broom and began very
gently to sweep it out, talking to it all the time.
"Come now, old fellow. I don't want to hurt you.
Shoo! Shoo on out." It was determined to stay in. I
suppose it was the first contact it had ever had with
human beings and didn't know how mean we could
be. It kept raising its head from the floor and trying to
dodge around my broom, first one side, and then the
other. I was persistent in giving him gentle little
sweeps, and finally succeeded in sweeping him out
and down the path. Coming back in, I went on with
my quilt tacking. Our work was now in the center of
the quilt and we had to stand in a stooping position to
tack it. We had been working steadily for about an
hour when I straightened up and without looking,
backed to my chair and sat down on something soft
and squirmy.

I jumped clear across the floor and let out another

bloodcurdling scream. There in my chair was that immense big gopher snake coiled round and round on the cushion of the chair, his head hanging over the edge as nonchalantly as though he really belonged there. And there sat Daddy on the front doorstep laughing with all his might. He said, "Remember, old lady! It's a gopher snake." I was standing there almost paralyzed with fear—cold chills running up and down my spine uttering exclamations of, "Oh! Ugh!" I was so angry with Daddy for laughing, for it's awful to be laughed at when you're as badly frightened as I was.

I picked up the chair and gingerly carried it to the back door, giving it a good hard jerk, and dumping the snake to the ground. Then I grabbed the broom and swatted him through the air ten feet at a swat. No gentle treatment this time. I got him outside the gate and down the gully, telling him he'd better stay there. When I came back into the house, Daddy was still chuckling. I looked at him belligerently and said, "If that thing comes back in here I'm gonna chop his head off. You just see if I don't!" With that I grabbed the darning needle and went furiously to work. All this time, my friend sat there with a smile on her face, but I think she was afraid to laugh out loud. When we finished the quilt it was noon and time to get dinner. When I reached into the woodbox for fuel for the cook stove, the piece of wood I pulled out held that horrible big gopher snake. By now my patience was exhausted. I screamed again, slamming him outside the door. Then I picked up a garden hoe and cut off his head, and carried him out into the sagebrush. When I came in, Daddy was still looking quite pleased. I shook my head at him and said, "A gopher snake may be a rancher's friend, but I'm not going to live in the same house with them."

"Well, old lady, that one did get a little too sociable. Maybe the rest won't be that friendly." That and one other, were the only gopher snakes we ever killed. We found they were truly the rancher's friend.

After the garden was planted and fenced, disappointment came. The greatest disappointment I ever had. My dear A.J. came down with one of his spells. I was so sure that fresh air and sunshine and rest would help him recover from his old malady. Maybe he had worked too hard, although he had gone at it slowly and rested often. Now here he was on the flat of his back, fighting for every breath he drew. My whole world fell around me, but we had to keep on. The cowboys came often to offer their help. One day they came with what they thought was a good suggestion. I took them in to A.J.'s bedside. The children, seeing company, followed us in. They stood around Daddy's bed, goggle-eyed and with open ears, taking in every word.

Pete, the cowboy boss, broached the subject. "Mr. Olds, there's a couple of unbranded yearling bulls up in the PF pasture. If you'll give us your branding iron, we'll put it on them for you." He then explained, "It's an unwritten law of the range that a leppy belongs to the first person to get his brand on it." A leppy is a long-eared, unbranded calf that in some way has been separated from its mother. They usually die of starvation or are killed by coyotes. Hence they belong to whoever claims them with his brand. I have heard a famous rodeo announcer crack the same old joke every year, "A leppy is a little calf whose ma has died, and whose pa has run away with another cow."

Branding leppies is legitimate business, but Daddy didn't think so.

He looked at the cowboys and said, "No, boys. Don't put my brand on those bulls. I know they're not mine. If my cow produces a calf—that's my calf. Otherwise, it's not mine." Then he went on, "I'll never be able to help the old lady and the children much, but I can at least help raise the kids to be honest. I'm not so good myself and wouldn't mind being a thief, but I'd hate damn bad to raise one. No, boys. Don't ever put my brand on a leppy."

Daddy might also have added that he was keeping the old lady honest too, for I thoroughly disagreed with him about branding leppies. I respected and believed in the law of the range. I wanted to brand leppies. I had charge of the branding iron and the cowboys would always help me, so why shouldn't I brand them? Because I couldn't live with an honest man who would think I was a thief. Though I was always good at spotting them, we never put our brand on one.

Daddy was bedfast that spell for weeks, and to make matters worse the three older children were riding Johnny one day, when he shied and all three fell off. Little Alice hit her shoulder on a rock, causing an abscess to form, and in a few days she was terribly sick. My home remedies were of no avail.

As if I didn't have troubles enough, Edson took down with a bilious spell. I didn't worry too much about him. He had just eaten too much sowbelly and beans, and I knew he'd be all right after a good vomiting spell. I was too worried over Daddy and Alice to be worried over him.

Alice tossed and moaned and screamed and was

running a high temperature. This had been going on for three days and was continuing into the third night. I had been sitting at her bedside all that time, and I couldn't stand it any longer. Something had to be done. I had to get her to a doctor, I told myself, or she would surely die.

While I didn't expect Daddy to last from one hour to the next and could do nothing for him, I could help little Alice. I think deciding what to do next was the hardest and most momentous decision I ever made.

Sara E. Thompson in Sonora, California, in 1898, a few
months before marrying A. J. Olds. (Photo courtesy of
Nevada Historical Society.)

Mom Olds on
the road to the
homestead,
about 1915.

Leslie, Martha, and burro Judy, 1915.

Original homestead, about 1915.

Family hay crew, about 1916.

Edson with trophy deer shot on Dogskin Mountain, 1917.

Jessie on Silver, about 1917. Note the costume.

Mom Olds and Leslie with bummers, 1919.

The enlarged homestead, 1923.

A. J. Olds, 1925.

Martha on Tule Peak monument, about 1927.

Mrs. Edson Olds in front of the homestead
with Edson's coyote skins, about 1930.

Mom Olds on Joe Hooker, 1943.

Six

I had to get Alice to the doctor. It was eleven o'clock at night when I decided, and our old horse was loose without hobbles and always very hard to catch. When we turned him loose we had to walk two miles and a half to the Winnemucca Ranch to get two cowboys to lasso him for us.

I have seen them run after him for hours and try in every way to fasten the loop on him. Johnny could dodge and slip through loops with the greatest of ease and skill. The boys would cuss and call him and his ancestors all kinds of names and finally succeed in catching him after hours of hard work.

When I went to A.J.'s bed and said, "I've got to take Alice to the doctor," it was small wonder that he gasped out, "Old lady, you're crazy. You'll never catch Johnny."

"Well, I'll go out and try. I can't let this baby die without trying to get help for her."

Johnny was running with a bunch of twenty gentle horses. I had glimpsed them earlier that evening feeding on a grassy flat about half a mile from our cabin. Hoping they were still there, I started out to find them.

Tying an old-fashioned apron around my waist, I filled my lap with grain, and armed only with the grain and a prayer, "Oh, God, help me catch old

Johnny," I walked out into the moonlight. Sure enough, the horses were still on the flat.

I approached them, talking low, "Come, boys. Come now. Don't be afraid," and rattled the grain in my apron. At their first sight of me they all turned and ran. I slowly followed, still talking and rattling the grain. Soon they turned and came toward me with mincing steps, snorting, their heads going up and down inquisitively, circling round and round me. I held out a handful of grain and kept on speaking to them softly. First one and then another took a taste of the grain as I held it out in my hand, then they all crowded around me, trying to get a handful of grain. All the while Johnny was sneaking along in the background. Had he seen a rope he would never have come near me. Seeing none, he came up from behind, put his head over my shoulder, and ate grain from my lap. I reached around with my free hand, untied my apron strings, and slipped them around his neck. I stood there letting him finish the grain and led him home. Any kind of a string would hold him, once he knew he was caught. I believe that was the only time he was ever caught without a wild chase. But also it was the only time he was ever caught with a prayer.

It took some time to get hitched up. Then I had to make Alice's bed in the wagon and put up a lunch for myself. It was two A.M. when I loaded my sick baby into the wagon. I kissed A.J. good-bye and started out with many misgivings.

I wondered if I was doing right. What if A.J. should die with Edson too sick to hold up his head, and only eight-year-old Jessie to take care of things. What would she do? It would frighten her to death if Daddy

passed away. All these and many other troubled
thoughts went through my mind. Why, I began to
wonder, had I undertaken such a thing? Why had I
thought I was so smart? Why had I thought I could do
what everyone told me couldn't be done? Why hadn't
I listened to them? With all these self-condemning
thoughts I drove the mile down to the gate that
opened onto the county road. When I closed the
heavy gate I was facing our cabin outlined so clearly
in the moonlight. It was then I had to truly decide
whether to go on or to turn back.

One minute I would think, "Yes, go on. Take Alice
to the doctor. Save her. I can't do anything for
Daddy." The next second I would think, "Don't leave
A.J. alone in there to die."

In sheer desperation I leaned my head on the top
board of the old gate and prayed, "Oh, God. What
shall I do?" My answer came in an almost audible
voice. "Do the best you can with the task you have at
hand." I decided the task at hand was getting my
baby to the doctor to save her life if possible. What a
relief it was to feel I was making the right decision. I
climbed into the wagon, hit old Johnny a crack, and
drove down the canyon.

The cool morning breeze felt good on my hot tired
brow. It was downgrade for the next few miles, and
old Johnny jogged along making pretty good time.
Soon the sun came up over Piute Ridge and, tired as I
was, I gazed in awe at the beauty of that early morning sunrise. I have passed there at sunrise many
times since and have never failed to stop and take in
the inspiring beauty. As I drove the sun came up in
redhot fury. By the time I reached Warm Springs and
the road turned upgrade the heat waves were al-

ready dancing along over the sage ahead of me like tall grain waving in the breeze. With old Johnny slowly clopping along in the sand, and with the sun beating on my weary back, it was then all my doubts and fears returned. Was I doing what was right? What had happened at home? I had been gone several hours. Was Daddy dead? It seemed the wagon wheels as they turned round and round were beating out the refrain, "What will I do, what will I do? What will the outcome be?"

Just then a strange thing happened. An old hymn popped into my mind right out of the blue sky. "What A Friend We Have In Jesus." I had sung it in church and Sunday school since early childhood, but it had been only words with a tune to them. Now they meant something. Those lines,

> We should never be discouraged,
> Take it to the Lord in prayer,

meant so much. I know God sent that hymn to comfort me. At first the words came slowly. I had forgotten most of them. It was with trembling lips that I started to sing, and soon all the words came back. I sang it loud and clear all the rest of the way up the sandy grade. There's a little secret there. You can't sing and worry at the same time. I sang! At last we reached the old Twenty Mile House where I could rest a few minutes, water the horse, make myself a cup of hot coffee, and eat my lunch. I hadn't eaten my breakfast before I left at two A.M. Now I was tired and hungry and oh, so sleepy. A cup of coffee would wake me up.

I watered the horse and went to look at Alice. She was asleep so I didn't disturb her. I gathered up some chips and laid them in the stove all ready to start a fire. It was then that I realized, to my dismay, that I was twenty miles from a match. Almost sick with disappointment, I ate my cold bread and butter, took a good drink of cold water, and drove on. I was feeling very sorry for myself at not having a cup of coffee. I was still sleepy and beginning to nod, and I feared I'd go to sleep and fall off the wagon. I reached Dry-Bone Lake where there was a long sandy hill going up out of Dry-Bone. I thought to myself, "It'll take Johnny fifteen minutes to climb that hill. I'll take a little snooze while he climbs to the top."

I drew Alice, still asleep, up under the shade of the wagon seat. I wrapped the lines around one wrist and stretched out on the seat, with one hand under my head as a pillow. I had Daddy's watch along with me and looked at the time. It was nine A.M. I had been on the road since two and had had no sleep for three days and nights. I must have slept the minute I laid my head down.

I awoke at two P.M. right in the same spot I had fallen asleep. The old horse had gone to sleep too! There he stood with his nose down to the ground, his knees bent, looking for all the world like the picture *The End of the Trail*. I had lain five hours in the hot June sunshine on that hot desert. It's a wonder I wasn't sizzled all the way through. As it was I had a big blister on my upturned face—the big, ugly, bubbly kind that looks like a kidney. My left eye was swollen shut, and, of course, I was suffering from the pain of the burns. Alice was still sleeping—the first real rest she had had for days.

I was provoked at the old horse for going to sleep. I now hit him a crack with the buggy whip, and he jogged along pretty lively for the rest of the way into town.

At that, it was five P.M. when we drove up to Dr. Pickard's office. I tied Johnny to a telephone pole in the alley, woke Alice and lifted her out of the wagon. It was now plain to see why she had slept so peacefully. The big abscess on her shoulder had broken open, and the corruption had run all over her. Her golden curls that I had made so carefully and lovingly that morning (while crying and thinking it would be the last time I'd ever make them) were now matted down from the fluid from the abscess. It was all over her little white dimity dress. What a spectacle we must have been. I looked as bad as she with my blister, my eye swollen shut, and my tear-stained, dusty face.

I hesitated, ashamed to go into the doctor's office, but there was nothing else to do. After resting my head on the wagon wheel and crying awhile, I picked up my courage, straightened my shoulders, and leading Alice by the hand, marched into the doctor's office defying the world to feel sorry for me.

Fortunately there was no one else in the office. The doctor was in the next room. He was not only the family physician, but an old family friend, as well. He came in and scarcely looking at Alice, stared at me. Then he put his arm around my shoulder and said, "Mrs. Olds, you're not going back to that homestead. You're trying the impossible. It's beyond human ability to go out there under your circumstances and make a living on an unimproved piece of land."

The doctor had been the strongest objector to our homestead plans. "Just forget this homestead scheme. Come on back into town. You and A.J. have lots of friends. We'll join together and help you raise those babies while A.J. tries to get well." He had told me two years before that there was nothing more he could do for A.J.

I pulled back from his arm saying, "Dr. Pickard, what in the world are you talking about? Of course I'm going back to that homestead just as soon as I can get there. Our school is established. We have our garden planted, and A.J. is much better off out there than he ever was in town. As for me, I just got silly and went to sleep out on the desert and burnt this big blister on my face, but it doesn't even hurt. I want you to look at Alice. She hurt her shoulder, so see what you can do for her."

He immediately turned his attention to little Alice, called his nurse and said, "Give her a bath." This she did, washing her hair and even her little dress and underslip. The doctor lanced her shoulder after giving her a slight anesthetic. While she lay there asleep her dress and slip dried and were ready to wear again.

After putting our horse up in the livery stable, we had supper and spent the night at the old Maddox Hotel, just a block from the stable. That is, we slept part of the night, for at two A.M. we started our homeward journey without any breakfast, for in those days you couldn't get anything to eat in Reno before six A.M.

Johnny plodded along pretty lively, and we arrived home at noon. And happy day! Both A.J. and Edson were up and out to meet us. Thus ended happily the most trying experience I ever had on the homestead. I knew right then the homestead would be a success, for nothing could ever happen that would seem any worse than that experience.

⧉[**Seven**]⧉

There are different tales about how Tule Mountain got its name. Legend has it that there was an old fellow named Tule Frank Henderson, on the Winnemucca Ranch at the base of a mountain.

This Tule Frank hauled hay that was full of tules, a kind of reed, and sold it in Virginia City in the early sixties. He would stop outside the city, walk in, and enquire which was bringing the highest price, hay or wood. Both were scarce. Then he would drive in and sell his load for whichever brought the highest price—wood or hay. Thus the mountain which he lived near came to have his name. Tule Frank is long since gone, but Tule Mountain remains a monument to his memory.

Speaking of monuments, there is one on top of Tule made of rocks. Some hunters started it by piling a few rocks together. Then they wrote their names and addresses and date of writing and placed the paper in a tobacco can on top of the pile of rocks. Some other hunters finding it, did the same, adding a few more rocks. Soon it became a kind of tradition. Everyone passing that way, hunters, cowboys, government engineers, and all, added a few stones and another name in the tobacco can.

The monument grew and the scroll of names out-

grew the tobacco can, and a five-pound baking powder can took its place. The can was always placed
directly on top of the monument, but everyone took
care to shelter it among the rocks so the wind
wouldn't blow it away.

When I last saw the monument it was eight feet
square at the base, rising in conical shape to a height
of eight feet, and it was four feet across at the top. On
excursions to the top of the mountain our children
and their friends would have their pictures taken
sitting on top of the monument.

After the advent of the automobile, sage hen hunters had access to the mountain and both the monument and the names on the scroll grew fast. There is
many a prominent name in the baking powder can on
top of Tule Mountain.

That next spring Hi returned from wintering in
town to his homestead to run in some wild horses. It
was great fun to watch him. He had built a round
stockade corral by setting long juniper posts, compact
and close together, two feet in the ground and seven
feet above. Then wiring them together close to the
top he had a good strong corral. He built two wing
fences running down hill, one to the east and one to
the south, forming a V opening into the corral. The
bottom of the opening was about half a mile wide.

Our cabin was at the lower end of this V. We would
climb on the roof and watch Hi singlehanded bring a
bunch of wild horses down off the mountain. He
headed them down toward the east, then circled
them out across the flat toward the opening of the
fence. Our cabin was just in the right place to turn
them into the mouth of the wing. We would dance up
and down on the roof and holler and whoop. Hi said

we helped him turn the horses, but we did it through sheer excitement. Once he got the horses inside the wing they were practically his. They had to run up through the V into his corral. We loved to watch him, for there is nothing more beautiful than wild horses running free and unfettered, their manes and tails flying in the breeze. Once they've had a rope on them they never again run with such free, easy grace.

We had little time to watch Hi, however, for the wood had to be brought down for the winter. The surrounding hills three miles away were covered with a heavy growth of juniper, which makes excellent fire wood, green or dry. That would be another long, hard job, for it would depend principally on A.J.'s health and failing strength.

We made picnics out of the wood trips. I put up a big lunch and everyone went. We could drive the first mile with the wagon. Then we had to unhitch old Johnny and put the pack saddle on him. It had irons fastened to it that hung down on each side of the horse. These irons were shaped like cradles, and made a good place for the two smallest children to ride. We hoisted little Leslie on one side, and baby Albert on the other. The rest of us walked, carrying the axes, the lunch, and a bucket of milk for the children. A.J. would chop with one axe, and I with the other. I had lots of strength, but it was surprising with how much more ease A.J. could fell a tree—the secret, of course, being that he could strike twice in the same place and I couldn't. The trees I felled were haggled down, but I came in mighty handy at packing the wood.

We would load the wood on the pack irons—each stick four feet long, for Daddy was very systematic in everything he did. The wood did pack better being of uniform length. When loaded, A.J. would tie it down, and I'd lead Johnny down to the wagon. After unloading the wood and getting it packed into the wagon, Johnny and I had the long two-mile hike back up the hill again, making a four-mile walk each trip. If we had a good day I walked sixteen miles, besides loading and unloading the wood. The picnic lunches were enjoyed by all. The children played, gathered flowers, and chased ground squirrels. Daddy chopped wood, resting a lot between times. We spent the whole summer long getting in our year's supply of wood.

One day as A.J. was in the hills chopping wood alone (I was at home washing) a friend drove out from town to see him on business. I told him Daddy was in the hills and wouldn't be down till five P.M., but that I would try to holler for him, and as sound always travels up, maybe I could make him hear.

I stepped outside, cupped my hands around my mouth and called, "Whoooooooohooooooo," several times.

I had always boasted of my penetrating voice. I became aware of it as a child. We used to call our stock and had a different call for each kind of animal. Our cow pasture was half a mile away, down a lane bordered on either side by corn fields. It was one of my jobs to bring in the cows. I would start down the lane singing, "Coooo, boss. Coooo, boss. Cooooo, cooooooo, cooooooo." The cows would always meet me at least half way.

For the horses we had an old bell mare named Bird. I would call, "Cope, Bird. Cope, Bird. Cooooop, cooooop, coop." Soon she would come with all the

other horses following her. Calling the pigs, however, was where I could shine. They ran in a twenty-
acre bluegrass pasture, but the pig pen was up by the
barn where we called them in and fed them twice a
day. I would sit on one of the tall posts in the pig pen
and call, "Puhoooey. Puhooey. Puhooooooooooey."
The pigs would all come squealing home. None of the
other children ever had the success in calling that I
had. It was a pity that they didn't give prizes for hog
calling in those days.

Now my hog calling voice came in handy on the
homestead. I "Hooooowhoooooed" several times
and then we sat down to wait, not knowing whether
he heard me or not.

Pretty soon here he came galloping down the hill
on old Johnny, thinking one of the children was hurt
or dead. I met him at the gate, telling him who was
there to see him. He stopped in his tracks looking
rather stern and then disgusted. Then he said, "By
George, old lady, your voice may have lost some of
its sweetness, but it hasn't lost any of its strength."
He was glad for my loud voice though, for it was
business of importance that the man wanted to see
him about. His woodchopping was interrupted for
the day, but I was glad to get him home early, for he
needed the rest.

We corded the wood in our back yard. A.J. was
very particular about cording it. Each rick had to be
four feet wide, four feet high, and eight feet long.
Those long ricks looked like a mountain of wood, but
we needed every stick of it, for the following winter
was one of the worst I have ever seen in Nevada.

About once a month our grub would run out, and I
would have to take three days off and make a trip to

town for supplies. The June and July food supply came from selling sage hens that Daddy would shoot for me. By August, the birds were feeding on sagebrush seeds, which made their meat bitter. Daddy balked. He would not shoot sagey birds for me to sell. He was honest all the way through. He'd just be damned if he'd sell anything he wouldn't eat himself. Grub was getting low and I was nagging a little, for I wasn't going to see the children going hungry. I told him he didn't need to sell them. I would take care of that part. All he needed to do was shoot them for me. He was adamant, however. No, sir! He wouldn't shoot one bird.

Then an unusual thing happened. It started to rain—something we never have in the summer in Nevada. It was a slow gentle rain—every drop going into the parched ground. It rained eight days, while our supplies got scarcer. We were beginning to tighten our belts and wonder. Then one morning the clouds cleared away, and the sun came out, red-hot as usual. The steam rose from the ground like a dense fog.

I began again, "Come now, Daddy. Go get us some birds. The children need food. I think we're justified in selling sagey birds to keep our family from going hungry."

Daddy said, "Well, old lady, I'll compromise. I'll go down and kill a few where they're feeding around the spring. Maybe they won't be sagey. You cook a few of them and if they're sagey and not fit to eat, we'll have to starve. I'll be damned if I'll kill any of them to sell." He very reluctantly took his gun and started out.

In a few minutes he came rushing back, bareheaded, his hat under his arm, shouting, "Look!

Look what I've got!" His hat was filled with mushrooms—big beautiful ones—the finest I have ever seen.

Mushroom spores lie dormant in the ground at all times, waiting for certain conditions to bring them up. That warm, gentle, eight-day rain had made perfect conditions for them to germinate. The entire countryside had popped up with mushrooms. We filled washbuckets, egg cases, dish pans, every conceivable container. They were the size of saucers, fully an inch thick, with the under side all pink and velvety. We were choosy in picking them. The finest grew under the black sagebrush where the leaf mold was six inches deep. We brushed away the leaf mold to get at the giant ones.

We loaded them into the wagon and away I went to town to sell them. I had never sold mushrooms, but I never doubted my ability to sell them. My only anxiety was in getting them to Reno in good condition. We had covered them over with our wagon canvas, and they were in perfect condition when I arrived.

The only sale I can remember was to a merchant on Commercial Row, who bought an egg case full and gave me ten dollars for it. The only reason I remember that sale is I have never seen that man at any time in the last forty years that he hasn't asked to buy mushrooms. Of course, that was the only time I ever had any to sell. I bought a wagon load of supplies and hurried home. I called that bill of grub my "Manna from Heaven".

By the latter part of September the mountain and valley quail were ready for market, and there were literally hundreds of both kinds. The sale of quail supplied us with food for both September and October. Then came November and the deer, which were in abundance all over the hills. With the sale of game we were never hungry.

Edson got his first deer that fall when he was eleven and felt he was quite grown up. After shooting it though, he felt sorry for it. It had looked beautiful bounding away in its fright, and then his gun had brought it down. When he cut its throat those pleading brown eyes looked up at him, and made him suddenly and unexplainably sad. Taking out his brown paper lunch bag, he sat down by the carcass of his deer and wrote this poem:

> In lieu of the law, in the book of reason,
> In lines plainly written I read,
> That murder is sport out of season
> With the price of the blood on your head.
>
> Now where can we hide the dead plunder
> That fell to our mischievous gun?
> And leave the wild forest to wonder
> At the spot where the murder was done.

He often said afterwards that he never killed a deer that he didn't feel sorry for. He didn't think much of the poem and would be surprised to know that Leslie still has it among her treasured keepsakes, on the same old brown paper bag that he wrote it on.

Eight

As there was an abundance of game in the country, it naturally followed that there were many predatory animals. There was usually a good market for the skins of coyotes and bobcats, besides the bounty of two and a half dollars per head.

If Edson could learn to trap, that would be another source of income. That fall he put in a few weeks with an old trapper. We bought him a couple of dozen of number three steel traps, and he very proudly and confidently set them out. A few days later he came running in all big-eyed and excited to tell me that he had caught a coyote in one of his traps. Would I come quick and help him skin it? He would kill it immediately, and we would skin it while it was still warm. The only knife we had was a dull butcher knife—I never owned any other kind.

Daddy had gone to town that morning with the only pocket knife we had in his pocket. I went with Edson to skin the coyote. He killed it with a club, while I turned my back and cried.

Then we started on our first skinning job. First we cut it up the belly, which was not the correct way. I would cut and skin for awhile, making too many slices in the hide, then Edson, thinking he could do better than I, would take the knife and try his hand.

All the time, one of us pulling as hard as possible on the hide. We made an awful mess of it.

Finally after three hours of hard work we got the hide off. It was full of holes. There wasn't a six inch square on the whole skin that wasn't cut. It might have been worth a few dollars when we started, but it wasn't worth ten cents when we finished. We had learned something, however. We had learned that we didn't know how to skin coyotes.

Edson went back to the trapper to learn the skill — and it is a skill — of skinning, in which Edson became very efficient. He learned to skin one in three minutes and often used to laugh at the three hours it had taken us on our first try. He became very good at trapping, and the income from his hides was our greatest help in early homestead days. That first year he sold one hundred and fifty dollars worth of raw skins.

We finished getting our wood down in November, and then we had to turn our attention to the school. We'd been wondering where we could get the money to buy the lumber needed for the schoolroom. Then a wonderful windfall came our way.

A wealthy sheepman below us gave us a miner's cabin that was on his property so we could tear it down and use the lumber to build our schoolroom. It was slow work as this cabin was five miles away. Daddy and Edson would drive down, work all day, and bring home a wagonful of lumber. After it was all hauled, we had the building to do. We added the extra room on the north end of our cabin.

Daddy had to do most of the work, for I wasn't much of a carpenter. The only nails I could ever hit with any accuracy were fingernails. He worked slowly along, but soon had to stop to celebrate our first Thanksgiving.

I had raised all eight of my little turkeys. When they were about three months old one of them got sick. It drooped around for days. I had given it grains of black pepper and all the home remedies I had ever heard of, but it looked like it was really going to die. I picked it up one day, and there seemed to be a rock in its craw the size of a walnut. I thought, "Well, the darn thing's going to die anyway. I'm going to open its craw and see what that is."

I plucked out a few breast feathers, got Daddy's razor, cut the outside skin of the craw, and then cut open the craw proper. There was the hard lump all right—as hard as a rock. It looked like grass matted down into a solid substance. I removed it, then with a sterilized needle and white silk thread I sewed up the craw and the outside skin. I then banded the turkey's leg for future reference. The turkey got well.

Now it was Thanksgiving time. I wanted to save two hens and a tom for next year's stock, which left me three to sell and two to eat—one for Thanksgiving and one for Christmas. I took good care to sell the banded turkey and was anxious to see what kind of scar the operation had left. Much to my surprise the skin was smooth—there was no scar. The operation had evidently been a perfect success. Then the day before Thanksgiving one of our remaining turkeys died. We had to make a quick decision as to whether to do without turkey for Thanksgiving or for Christmas. We decided to have our turkey dinner on Christmas, for that's what the children wanted. We had already invited the cowboys and old Goshie, the foreman of the sheep ranch for dinner. Goshie, a

French Basque whose real name was Juan Barrandegui, was a big fat fellow with a stomach that hung over the edge of his trousers, which he constantly tried to pull up. He had a kind old face with almost liquid brown eyes. He thought the world of the children and I never went to town without Goshie sending some money along with me so that I could buy a special treat for them.

We had to have something special for dinner, so Daddy went out and killed a number of mountain quail. We all feasted on stuffed, roasted quail and never missed the turkey.

Edson took the dead turkey for coyote bait, wired it to a juniper tree across the flat and caught three coyotes with it. The coyotes ate all the flesh off the bird, but it was years before the ligaments disintegrated and let the bones drop. Now after half a century has passed the leg bones of that turkey are still wired to the juniper tree.

With Thanksgiving over, we turned back to the building of the schoolroom. We built it twelve by fourteen feet. It was to be a schoolroom from nine A.M. till four P.M., and the teacher's private room for the rest of the time. We moved in seats and blackboards from the other side of the district. There was a three-quarter bed and a closet in one corner with a curtain drawn around them for privacy. We installed a small table for the teacher's desk. As Daddy had several bad spells that interrupted our work, it was just a few days before Christmas when we finished our school.

Daddy had to go in right after Christmas to find a teacher, so we didn't go in for Christmas supplies. I made new outfits for the three little girls' dolls. The baby was too young to know about Christmas, and Daddy took care of Edson's present by giving him his pocket knife. The cowboys came for dinner and brought candies, nuts, and oranges, and we had some shiny red apples stored in the cellar. We had raised popcorn the previous summer, which we popped and strung to decorate the tree. Daddy took all the children with him across the flat to choose a juniper for our Christmas tree. This started a tradition. My children to this day would rather have a juniper than the most beautiful blue fir. They chose one with lots of blueberries hanging from the branches. We had candles and some lovely old candlesticks. When our tree was set up and decorated with bright red apples, oranges, strings of popcorn, bags of candy, and candles, the children thought it the most beautiful tree they had ever seen.

Daddy got up early Christmas morning, lit the fire in the stove, lit the candles, and then rang the school bell announcing, "Come, kids. Old Santy's been here."

The cowboys and old Goshie all came for dinner. We ate our remaining turkey. We had the traditional dinner with turkey, mince pies, and all the trimmin's except the cranberry sauce.

It was soon January, and winter was upon us. We had a good supply of wood, our cellar was full of vegetables and canned fruit (I had put up six hundred quarts of canned goods from the fruit that our two big neighboring ranches had given us) and dozens of bottles of jelly and jam. I mean bottles literally. I had no jelly glasses, but we had collected beer bottles from the surrounding countryside, and I had converted them into jelly glasses. I soaked a string in coal oil, and tied it around the bottle where I wanted it to break. Then when the string was burned and the bottle doused in a bucket of cold water, it would break evenly where the string was tied. In that way I always had a supply of jelly glasses.

There was an abundance of meat in the hills, for deer were plentiful and apparently tame. They stalked past our cabin as if we weren't there. We had, besides, the one hundred and fifty dollars in gold that I kept in an old, cracked pitcher on the pantry shelf. That cracked pitcher was our bank for a good many years.

The gold I had was a hundred-fold gain over the one dollar and fifty cents that I had when we arrived on our place.

Now we were all ready for our trip to town to get the school teacher and our supplies. We debated which one should go. I decided on Daddy, as he was a well educated man and better qualified to choose a school teacher than I. In our ignorance, we acted as though teachers grew on trees and all we had to do was pick one, never realizing that in January teachers were employed, and we would be very fortunate to find one. Then the gods of the weather took over. The wind blew in hurricane force for three days. Then the storm broke. It snowed and blowed, and the snow drifted for three or four days—the worst storm and the coldest winter I have ever seen in Nevada. When the skies cleared we found ourselves surrounded with three feet of snow. There was no handy airlift to drop food to us or to our stock. There we were snowed in and the thermometer stood at thirty below. Whether we survived or not was up to us. If I ever gain any fame in this world it'll be for proving the survival of the fittest. We lived where we should have starved.

Fortunately we had made arrangements with our neighboring sheepman to pasture our surplus stock of two cows and three calves. We had only one milk cow and the horse to feed at home. Our hay crop from our eight acres of meadow had been stacked for us in the PF haystack. The foreman had intended to haul it up to us later as we needed it. But our hay was a mile away and three feet of snow on the ground made it difficult to get to it. Besides Daddy had had words with the PF foreman and he now claimed we had no hay. Our problem was to get that hay up to the horse and cow to keep them alive.

It is truly said, "Necessity is the mother of invention." I got no patent on my invention, but I did find a way to get our hay hauled. We had bought half a ton of wheat for the chickens in the fall, storing it in a tin-lined bin. I took the grain sacks, which had held the wheat, ripped them open and sewed together one big bag, four feet wide and eight feet long. This bag, when crammed full and tight with hay would hold a hundred pounds. We put the pack saddle on Johnny, and then placed the big sack over the pack saddle for a blanket. Then Edson and I climbed on and rode very slowly through three feet of snow down to the haystack a mile away. We made these trips at night so the foreman wouldn't see us. The hay was ours, of course, but we had to steal it to get it. We'd fill our bag, cramming it down tight, then tie it securely to the saddle with ropes. Then we'd lead old Johnny to a long, low hanging branch of a nearby tree, which stood right at the end of the hay corral. Edson would hold the horse while I climbed the tree, crawling out

on the branch that was just barely high enough to
miss the hay. I would get down on the sack of hay
and pick up the reins to hold Johnny steady while
Edson would crawl down on the sack behind me.

It was a wobbly, precarious position. Sometimes
one of us would fall off, only to rise and flounder
through the deep snow, fall again, and finally grab-
bing Johnny's tail we would manage to make it to the
corral at home. It was impossible to get back on, once
we got away from that friendly tree.

By making our hay trips every other night, we were
able to keep our animals alive through the long, cold
winter.

As I sat up there, swinging and swaying on the
haysack, three feet above the back of our tall, bony
old horse, I was reminded of my childhood's ambi-
tion to ride an elephant. The big circuses all came to
our home of Ottumwa, Iowa. The Ringling Brothers,
Barnum and Bailey, the Fourpaw Brothers, in fact all
of them, used to hit our town. How we children used
to devour with our eyes the gay posters that were
plastered all over the country barns. On circus day we
got up before sunup, father would hitch up the team
to our big lumber wagon, pile us all in, and away we
would go to the circus.

In those days there was always a parade of the
animals through the streets—some in closed cages,
but many of them parading loose. The parade was
always advertised to start promptly at ten A.M., but it
never came till one P.M. The streets would be lined on
both sides with people, big, little, old and young, all
leaning out into the street, craning their necks for the
first sign of the parade. The big blue-garbed policemen on their prancing steeds rode back and forth,

waving their sticks, and pushing the crowds back to the sidewalk. This seemed a useless effort, for as soon as the policemen passed, the crowd would surge again out into the street. Finally, after what seemed an endless time, someone would yell, "Here she comes!" That yell would echo all down the street.

The old calliope would come into view first, drawn by six beautiful, prancing white horses, their necks arched, and their harnesses and bridles adorned with great, red tassels. We children thought the calliope made the sweetest music in the world. But how we loved the huge elephants! I would gaze in awe at the beautiful lady in the grand, flowing robe, sitting way up there in the little box atop the animal, swinging and swaying to the rhythm of the elephant's clumsy strides. He was always garbed in a bright, gold trimmed, purple robe. How I envied that lady way up there in her box saddle. Someday, I promised myself, I would do the same. I would join a circus when I grew up and learn to ride an elephant.

Now in our haylift trips I was surely getting all the rhythm of the swing and sway, minus the elephant in his magnificent robes, and the beautiful flowing gown. But it was all great fun. We laughed a lot and fell off often.

Our horse and cow were plentifully supplied with feed, but as time went on we began to wonder how we were going to make out, and if we had enough staples to hold out till we could get into town. All "boughten" supplies were gone when the storm started. I had had a list a yard long written out for Daddy to buy when he went to town to get the teacher. Now first one thing and then another vanished. First our sugar.

"No sugar?" asked Daddy. He made a terrible fuss, not having sugar for his coffee. That want was soon eliminated, for we soon had no coffee to put sugar in. Then the salt went, which I missed more than anything we had to do without. Next the lard was gone, and we had no fat of any kind.

Our neighbor homesteaders, Tom Speers and John Green, had two good, strong saddle horses. When the storm first ended they decided to ride to town. They stopped at our place and gave us what scant supplies they had. The plan was this: One of them would stay in town and give up his horse to use as a pack animal. The other was to buy a big bill of grub and bring it out to us. We gave them one of our precious twenty-dollar gold pieces. Although we were snowed in we anticipated no discomfort for ourselves, for Tom or John would be back in a few days with our provisions. Since we had fruit, vegetables, and meat, we could get along for awhile without any "boughten" supplies. Vegetables without seasoning are not good, so we quit cooking them, for they are better raw without salt. We had lots of flour, for we had laid in a ton early in the fall. It was in sacks wired to the rafters around the house to keep it away from the mice. I baked light bread and was very careful to keep my jar of potato yeast fresh, as we had no salt, grease, or baking powder to bake any other sort of bread. I believe the human body needs quantities of fat, for we all longed for fat of some sort. We had plenty of deer meat, but there was no fat on it. I had two dozen old hens that I was keeping for next year's stock. I began to kill one a week and by gleaning every bit of gut fat would get a cup full of fat from each chicken. I made gravy thickened with a spoonful of flour, and spread the hot gravy over a thick slice of bread. When we had this gravy it was the only time we would sit at the table to eat. Other times we would open the top of the stove to grill our slice of venison, lay it hot and dripping between two slices of bread, stand there by the stove with a venison sandwich in one hand, a raw carrot or turnip or chunk of cabbage in the other, and top it off with a dish of canned peaches, pears, or plums. That was our bill of fare for breakfast, dinner, and supper for the next ten weeks.

About a week after the boys went to town we began to wonder what had become of them and the supplies that we had given them money to buy. Then one night about ten o'clock we heard John coming up through the meadow, shouting, shooting, and hollering. We thought he must be either drunk or crazy. He proved to be both!

Tom had given John the money to buy our food, and John had spent it in a saloon where he lay drunk several days. The saloon keeper owned a pet monkey, which had bitten two of John's fingers causing infection to set in. When he finally sobered up enough to think of our plight and the bill of grub he was to buy for us, he bought what he had money enough to buy. He saddled up his horse and came out with our provisions. When he reached our place he was delirious with pain and fever and had a bad case of blood poisoning. The provisions that he brought us consisted of fifty cents worth of coffee and a flask of whiskey.

We were terribly disappointed, but we had no time to think of it, for a man's life was in danger. We had to work fast if we were to save him. I had a ten-pound sack of Epsom salts that the cowboys had supplied

me with to doctor one of their sick horses. We put a
wash boiler full of water on the stove, emptying in all
the salts that would dissolve. We got old John to bed
on the couch in the kitchen, but we had a hard time
holding him there in his delirium. After stripping off
his outer clothing, we had to cut his undershirt at the
sleeves to get it off him. His arm was swollen and
discolored almost to the shoulder. There were ugly
red streaks running from the wrist up. When the
water was hot we set the boiler on the floor beside
him, immersing his arm in it. We had an extra pan of
hot salts water on the stove to reinforce the water in
the boiler as it cooled. At last John quieted down and
went to sleep, but Daddy and I worked steadily on
with him until daylight. By then the discoloration and
the angry streaks had all left his arm.

When he awoke next day at four P.M. he was peni-
tent and much embarrassed. He was a fine old fellow
when sober. He saddled up and left as soon as possible much to our great relief, for one more horse to
feed from our precious hay and one more human
being in our close quarters would really have been the
last straw.

We knew now there would be no relief for us, so
we had to strengthen our determination and pull
through the best way we could. We had an abundance of our home supplies, but we wondered how
long we could live on that kind of diet.

After about six weeks of our fare we began to break
out with some kind of a rash. We were terribly worried. A.J. and I would lie awake nights wondering if it
could be some lack in our diet that was causing us to
break out. We weren't sick or feverish—only itchy
and uncomfortable. What could it be? Could we be
getting scurvy? We had read of men at sea getting

scurvy from an improper diet. Perhaps that's what
we had. We looked the word up in the dictionary
without getting much enlightenment on the matter. It
said, "Covered or affected with scurf or scabby". We
weren't scabby but only itchy. We had scratched the
hide off in numerous places. Maybe it was the itch.
Round and round we went, fearing something, we
knew not what.

When the storm first ended we cleared the snow
from a place about twelve feet square on the south
side of the house. With the building sheltering this
cleared place on the north and with the snow banked
high on the other three sides, the clearing made a
comfortable place to sit or play, especially from eleven A.M. to two P.M., when the sun was shining
directly down into it. We bundled up and spent all
three hours out in the sunshine every day.

One day while A.J. and the children were out in the
sun I was in the house washing, bending over an
old-fashioned tub and board and the steamy hot
suds. Surely I had felt something crawling across my
chest. I opened the front of my dress and my woolen
undershirt, (we all wore woolen underthings and
needed them badly) and sure enough, there was a
small, gray insect of some kind crawling across my
chest. I picked it up between my thumb and finger
and went out to where A.J. and the children were.

"Look, Daddy. What is this? I picked it off my
chest."

He looked. "Hell, old lady. It's a grayback."

"Well, what's a grayback?" I had never heard of
one.

"Why, it's a louse! Old lady, you're lousy!"

"Well, then," I decided, "That's what's the matter
with all of us."

"No, sir," said Daddy. "I've been lousy lots of

times in mining camps. That's not what ails me."

We were all broken out on the wrists. Daddy rolled back his shirt sleeve, turning back the cuff of his undershirt, and sure enough! He was alive with lice. The great mystery was solved. We were all lousy, even the two-year-old baby.

How any decent, clean family could become so lousy without knowing it is a mystery to me. Old John had left his calling card. Before coming out he had lain on the floor of the saloon and had picked up the lice. The night he stayed at our house he had left a few of the seed on the bed.

It was a relief to us to learn that we were only lousy, after fearing such terrible things as scurvy and itch and we knew not what, but it was awful to endure the crawling and itching for the next twenty-four hours till our clean clothes got dry. We had to dry them over the stove and kept a roaring fire going day and night so as to dry them as soon as possible. Then we all took baths with plenty of sheep dip in the water.

I had no disinfectant to put in the wash water, so I boiled all our clothing in sheep dip and kerosene. It didn't take us long to get deloused once we found out our trouble.

Life had to go on in the same monotonous way till the snow melted, but our courage and our morale were good. Not one of us was sick a day in all the long, cold winter. Perhaps most of our human aches and pains are caused by overindulgence. We were never comfortably warm and never overstuffed, for the food without seasoning of any kind didn't taste good enough to cause us to overeat.

The snow began to disappear slowly, and on the

seventeenth of March, we had been snowed in just ten weeks. A.J. hitched up the wagon and went to town to get our long-delayed provisions and the new school teacher.

§[**Nine**]§

Someone has said, "Where ignorance is bliss, 'tis folly to be wise." In our case it was when ignorance is bliss it is a blessing. That winter of 1910-11 when we were snowed in, the Shoshone Indians went on their last warpath. They came down into Nevada from Southern Oregon and killed a few isolated ranchers. When they were finally stopped they were only about fifty miles north of us.

We would very likely have met the same fate, but word of the uprising got to the Washoe County sheriff in Reno. He made up a posse of about fifty picked men and wiped out the ravaging warriors. There was one young squaw with a little papoose, whom they were bringing into the Washoe jail the day A. J. arrived in town for supplies. He had gone to the jail to dispose of some coyote scalps and heard the whole story. Had we known of that uprising while we were snowed in, we would surely have had some sleepless nights.

Washoe County had a hard time deciding what to do with the little squaw and her papoose. After keeping her for several months they finally sent her back to her tribe in Oregon.

When Daddy returned he had a broken-down miner to teach our school. True, he was a Yale graduate and had no trouble in getting a permit to teach. If our children had been in high school he might have been satisfactory, but he was too highly educated and his talk went over their heads. After teaching for a month, he realized that he was a failure and resigned.

This time it was my turn to choose a teacher. I'd gained some confidence in myself, and anyway I couldn't do any worse than Daddy had. It was now April and there was beautiful spring weather. Luck was with me in getting a teacher. A big German girl, Elsie Von Dornam, who had just finished her seven months' school term down at Bullfrog, an old mining camp in the southern part of the state, had reported to our school superintendent that she would like to have another short term of school if she could get it. I had asked the superintendent's help in getting a teacher, and he sent me to see her.

I told her that our school was isolated and that she might not like it out there. She thought she would, for she was young and just beginning her teaching career. She would be glad to come. She had lots of courage or she never could have made that trip. Our old horse had gotten sick on the way out. They had fed him alfalfa hay at the livery stable, which had given him colic. We had gone only three miles when I had to unhitch him, remove the harness and let him roll. After he rolled and groaned and I led him around for awhile, I hitched him up again and we slowly crept along. All that thirty-five miles he was so sick he could scarcely pull the wagon. I unhitched him frequently and let him roll. The last seven miles from home the going was heavy because of the upgrade. We always dreaded that last, long pull.

I consoled myself with the thought, "Well, he can't

go any slower when we reach the grade than he has all the way out." I was mistaken. The first step he took upgrade he stopped and wouldn't pull a pound. There we were with a heavy load on the wagon, it was sundown, and we were seven miles from home. What to do next? I knew I could easily walk that seven miles, but I hesitated to ask the new teacher to do so. I tactfully said, "I'll walk five miles up to the sheep ranch and get another horse. Then I can come back and get you and the wagon." Just then a coyote let out a howl. It frightened Miss Von Dornam. Evidently she had never seen a coyote or heard one holler.

"Oh, no, I'll walk with you. I can make it if you can."

I unhitched Johnny and led him slowly along. When we reached Warm Springs Creek, which is usually a dry wash on the desert, it was a raging torrent two hundred feet wide, fed by the melting snow from the hard winter. We took off our shoes, stockings, and panties, rolled up our dresses around our waists and stepped into the ice cold water. Miss Von Dornam got across first. In the middle of the stream old Johnny stopped to drink. He'd drink awhile, then lift up his head, yawn, and drink again. This went on for nearly fifteen minutes, with me standing waist deep in the icy water, dancing and jumping up and down. My limbs were almost paralyzed. Teacher was on the opposite bank, clapping her hands and laughing, and saying, "Oh, if I only had a camera, if I only had a camera!"

After what seemed an endless time to me, Johnny decided to let me lead him across the creek. On the other side of the creek, Miss Von Dornam and I sat down and dried our feet on my petticoat. She was a real Pollyanna. "I'm so glad I had to wade that icy stream," she said, "Otherwise I might never have known the full benefit of a cold footbath."

The dear girl, I learned later, always found something to be happy about. It was surprising how rested and refreshed we were after our half-immersion in the icy stream. We were fortified for the rest of our walk.

We reached the sheep ranch and old Goshie at about nine P.M. I never used his real name, and I don't know how he came by such a nickname. He welcomed us warmly, calling the teacher "school mama," prepared a good, hot supper for us consisting of lamb chops, fried potatoes, and sheepherder's sour bread. First though, we fixed up a bottle of baking soda and water and poured it down old Johnny. Then we turned him loose in the corral and hoped for the best.

Next morning the horse was all right with no hangover from yesterday's colic. I roade him to our wagon on top of the harness, hitched up, and drove back to pick up Miss Von Dornam.

We arrived home at noon where they were all anxiously awaiting us, as we were twenty-four hours late. I realized that I had picked a winner of a school teacher. She had shown fortitude and uncomplaining courage, and I knew that trip must have been something of a hardship to a young girl, thoroughly unfamiliar with the desert. She proved her worth. Our children had missed a whole year's schooling except the month when the miner had taught them nothing. She worked everly and late with them, giving them homework and helping them with it in evenings. By working diligently, she brought them all through their year's work by the first of July.

Little Albert, who was only two and a half years old, loved Miss Von Dornam and wanted to go to school with the other children. In warm weather, when the schoolroom door was left open, the baby would play in front of the door. One day Miss Von Dornam, to keep him from disrupting lessons, told him to go out and catch a butterfly for her, never dreaming that he could catch one.

He was chubby and slow, but he worked for hours, toddling along after them out in the sagebrush. Finally, right in front of the schoolroom door he caught one. I was out hanging clothes, when I heard him saying gleefully, "Caught a butterfye for teacher. Caught a butterfye." I turned and saw him start toward the schoolroom door with a beaming face. Just then a turkey ran to meet him and grabbed the butterfly from his hand. The ecstatic look on his face changed in an instant to one of grief. Miss Von Dornam, who had been watching him through the open door, gathered him up in her arms saying, "This dear baby has earned a day in the schoolroom."

Catching "butterfyes" for Miss Von Dornam became a must for Albert from that time on, and they were bothered no more with him, for he never caught another one.

When our state school superintendent visited our school he told me that Miss Von Dornam was one of the best educators Nevada had ever known and not to expect her with her talent and ability to be wasted on our little schoolroom another year. But we were always especially blessed in securing good teachers. We kept them only a year, however, as our little school was always a stepping stone for them to something better.

Now that our school was going, the big sum of twenty dollars a month which was coming in for the teacher's board would more than buy our groceries for the whole family for nine months of the year. Mrs. Benoist's plans had worked out well, and after she sold her place we fell heir to the whole district and had school for nine months instead of five.

This was our second year on the homestead and it began to look more and more like a success.

In June Daddy went into town for supplies and miraculously met my brother, Dave, who was combing the town looking for some trace of me. He lived in Australia, and I hadn't heard from him in many years. He had been back to Chicago on business, and while visiting our relatives in Iowa had heard that I was living in Reno, Nevada. He was lucky enough to meet Daddy on the trip in. Dave didn't have time to come out with our slow horse and wagon, so he rented a livery team and surrey and he and Daddy started out. They arrived at ten P.M. We were all in bed, and I hadn't expected A.J. till the next day. I heard A.J.'s voice, then—hark! I heard a voice out of the past. Strange how the memory of a voice stays with one over the years. I jumped out of bed barefooted, and clad only in my nightgown, I ran out of doors crying, "Davey, Davey! Where in the world did you come from?"

"From the other side of the world," he said. "Down under as we Australians call it."

We talked till after midnight, when he had to get a little sleep; he was catching a train next day for San Francisco, then the boat for Australia. He had only a few hours to spend with me. We put him to bed with Edson on the lounge in the kitchen. He was up next morning at daybreak and went to stand on a little rise in front of the house to look over the layout. I, not wanting to miss a minute's visit with him, got up and followed him out. We stood there on the hill together looking over the place. How he must have pitied me with all my little children, a semi-invalid husband and an unimproved homestead. I didn't think so then, for in my mind I could see the place differently. I visioned green alfalfa fields, big haystacks, and great herds of cattle roving over the hills. I felt sure he could see them too.

Dave was a self-made man. He had gone to work for the Diamond Drill Company of Chicago when he was a lad of thirteen as a chore boy and had steadily risen in worth till now he owned a fourth interest in the company's Australian holdings and was their general manager over there, including Australia, Tasmania, and New Zealand. I knew Davey would see things my way.

I proudly asked, "Well, Dave. What do you think of the layout?" It was a bold question, and I wanted a true answer, but I wanted his answer to be what I wanted it to be! Surely he would give me some encouragement.

He drew himself up and said, "Well, Sadie, if you have the guts to stay with it, you'll make good. But by God, it'd take Mammy's own grit to do it."

I almost duplicated my mother's life. She had raised nine children on a farm with a semi-invalid husband.

Then Davey offered, "I'll loan you money to buy cattle, farm implements, or anything you need to make a success of the ranch. I've plenty of money, and it would be a great pleasure to me to help you now. You can repay me later."

My false pride kept me from accepting his offer. I would have none of it. Our place was not a success as yet, and if it failed I wanted to be the only loser. He smiled and I think he was proud of me, for he said, "If you ever do get to a place where you need help, let me know."

What a wonderful backbone that put in my plans. It was great to know and feel that I could always get help if I needed it. The offer was always my "ace in the hole."

Dave left about ten o'clock that day, and upon leaving he pressed a paper bill into the baby's hand, which I supposed was a dollar. When I looked later, I found it to be a hundred dollar bill.

Ten

During the next spring and summer many unexpected things happened. That year the PF outfit bought a bunch of new purebred bulls and turned them in the field around our house. They hadn't removed the old bulls yet, and it was many a bullfight we witnessed. Most of them were just minor little scraps with lots of bawling and dirt pawing but with no real fighting. But there were two big fellows of about equal size and strength who got to fighting in earnest, and we saw an example of the law of the survival of the fittest.

They fought for three days and nights, and we could hear them bellowing at all hours and then coming together in a loud crash. After the three days of constant fighting, one of them began to weaken. The stronger one, seeing his advantage, pressed it, never allowing his opponent to rest, but keeping him constantly on the move by prodding him with his horns. When the weak one fell from exhaustion the big fellow would bellow, paw the dirt, hook him, and then walk away to eat and drink. Always he kept his eye on the fallen animal and if that bull so much as moved, the victor would charge him again. He would have kept the other there until he died if we had not come to the rescue. Up until the time the bull fell, we had enjoyed the show immensely, but now that he was down we knew he couldn't live if that treatment kept up. We sent one of the children to the Winnemucca Ranch to call for help. The cowboys soon came and drove the victorious bull away, thus ending our three days' show.

That spring the big PF outfit got conscience stricken at having so much unpatented land fenced. They had all their land surveyed and tore down miles of old fence, rebuilding on their newly surveyed lines. This threw hundreds of acres of grazing land out on the open range, including our homestead.

Now that we were out in the open with no fence around us, we had to get busy. There was lots of work to be done. First we had to fence our land, then build a cross fence to protect our meadow. There were still plenty of juniper trees in the hills that would make good fence posts, but as always, it was slow work getting them out. Daddy went to the hills to cut the posts, then on Saturday and Sunday I could leave the baby with the older children and the teacher and snake the posts down where we could drive to them with a wagon. Then we borrowed a big wagon and team to haul them down. Dave's one-hundred-dollar present to the baby paid for fencing our land with good three-strand barbed wire.

Our little herd was increasing. Dairies in Reno were giving away newborn calves, and with each trip to town that I made during the summer I brought home one or two calves—whatever number we had enough milk to feed. I had gathered up three such calves our first summer on the homestead and those with our own three were ready to brand. I wanted to call on the cowboys to help us, but Daddy would have none of that. No, we would brand them ourselves. If we were going to be cattlemen, we couldn't depend on the cowboys to come and do our branding.

We went to work and built a willow corral. When finished it was a circle about fifty feet in diameter with the fence about six feet high. We then set good strong posts firmly in the ground at opposite sides of the enclosure. Not having a horse to lasso and brand from, these were to be our snubbing posts. We picked out a good, fat bull calf for our first branding victim. Neither of us was skilled at the work. We had both seen branding done but always with a well trained cow pony. Now we would have to do our branding on foot. The calves were gentle, and it wasn't necessary to lasso them.

I walked up to the biggest one and put the rope around his neck while Daddy put the rope around his heels. We downed him, stretched him out between the two posts and tied him hard and fast. I headed him down while A.J. worked on the other end. As soon as I sat down on the calf, I could see we were choking him.

I hollered, "Cut the rope, quick, Daddy! We're choking him!"

A.J. drawled slowly, "Old lady, you sit there till I tell you to get up."

I sat, but I bawled loud and furiously the whole time. Having finished, Daddy said, "Now, you can get up." I did, but the calf didn't. We had choked him to death.

It wasn't a complete loss, however. We dressed him; hung the carcass up on a swing, and that night at midnight, when the animal heat had left the body, I hitched up Johnny and drove to town to sell my first veal. We had learned something. We knew we couldn't brand calves. Thereafter, we always had the cowboys come and help us with our branding.

That summer our neighbor, Tom Speers, who had homesteaded the same year we did, passed away. He had made quite a few improvements on his place. He had built a cabin, fenced his land, and had about ten acres of alfalfa and wheat. He hadn't "proved up" on his land as yet, and being unmarried, his property went to his mother, who lived back in Nebraska. We bought his homestead right from her, paying two hundred dollars for it. As A.J. had already used his homestead right, we filed a desert claim on Tom's land. At that time you could acquire three hundred and twenty acres of land under the Desert Act if the land adjoined yours. The conditions were that one had to develop water for irrigation, enough to raise a crop and improve the property.

Our homestead and all the land surrounding it was hilly and steep. There was a small spring that came to the surface high up on a hill on this desert land. Daddy's knowledge of mining engineering stood us in good stead. He calculated he could go down the hill three hundred feet, run a tunnel one hundred and sixty feet into the hill under the spring and tap the water at a ninety-foot depth. This would more than double the flow of the water. Then we broke the new land, planting and irrigating several new acres of alfalfa that spring. With this increase in our hay crop we were far ahead of our increase in cattle, and we wouldn't have to worry about hay for a few years.

That year Edson sold six hundred dollars worth of skins, most of which we spent for badly needed farming equipment such as a hay rake, plow, wagon, mowing machine—in fact, every implement that is needed on a ranch. It is surprising how many different things we had been borrowing. We had to save some of the six hundred to pay for the baby which was on its way, and which was to be born in September of 1912.

That same summer the Southern Pacific built a short-line railway between Fernley, Nevada, and Klamath Falls, Oregon, cutting off a three-hundred-mile haul from Oregon to points east. I'll show you how these two great events dovetailed and came together.

Seventy miles of this roadbed ran through the Pyramid Lake Indian Reservation, and of course, there wasn't a saloon allowed within five miles of the reservation line.

The Twenty Mile House had burned down in 1911, but the county had kept up the well as long as there was any horse and buggy travel. Now an old madam from Sacramento, with an eye to business, came up and leased the Twenty Mile House site. She put up a saloon, built some cribs, and installed a group of prostitutes. They did a land office business from the start. There were six-hundred men on the road crew and there was always a bunch of them willing to walk the sixteen miles to the roadhouse for entertainment. They would get drunk, stay till they spent their paychecks, and then walk back—there was no other transportation.

All that summer before my baby was born I hated to pass the new Twenty Mile House. There were drunks of all description lying around—dead drunks, shoot-em-up drunks, and happy drunks. None of them ever molested me in any way, although the porch of the saloon came out over the well curb, and when I went to draw water for my horse I was half-way in the saloon door.

One morning one of the girls came out and talked to me. It was the only time I'd ever knowingly talked to a prostitute, and I felt disgraced for life. Afterward I was glad I'd had that conversation with her, though it was mostly one-sided, for she did all the talking.

Daddy was so afraid our baby would be born on the mountain with him for midwife—I think that's where the shoe really pinched—that he ushered me off to town a full month before the baby was due. While he was urging me to go, a friend of ours came out in a brand new car, which made a convenient way in for me without Daddy having to hitch up the wagon and take me in, leaving the children alone for three days.

It was the first time our friend had ever driven a car without the instructor along, and our road from the Twenty Mile House out was very poor; in fact, it was almost impassable for a car. Some motoring enthusiast had erected a sign at the forks in the road, pointing our way. It read, "From here on this road is only a cow trail, and a damn poor one at that."

Our friend was so afraid that the old stork would catch up to us that he tried to drive carefully. At the foot of each hill was a wash with little gullies crossing the road. Our friend would shift into low, go slow, kill his engine, back down, get out and crank up, and start all over again with the same result. Then on the third try he'd get angry, swear a little, and turn on lots of gas, which would take us bumpity-bump to the top. This performance was repeated at each hill, but we finally arrived at the maternity hospital all in one piece.

I had been there a little over a month when my

baby girl was born. We named her Martha, and she was the first baby I'd ever had who was issued a birth certificate immediately after her birth. It was three weeks before I had a chance to go home, as A.J. was reluctant to leave the children alone to come after me, so he waited for me to get a chance ride.

That fall Hi was building a barn, and he had come in for a four-horse load of lumber. He called me up the night before he left for home saying, "If you think you're strong enough to ride home on a load of lumber you can ride out with me tomorrow."

I stood there with the phone in my hand, "Oh, yes! I'm strong enough. I can make it. I'll go, Hi."

"Hold on a minute now. I have a heavy load and can't make it all in one day. I'll have to stop at the Twenty Mile House. I have my bedroll, that I can roll out under the wagon, but what in hell will I do with you and the baby?"

I stood dancing from one foot to the other, thinking "What will I do? What will I do?" I wanted to get home so badly. I knew my children needed me, as their father was never very apt at taking care of them. Besides it was now the middle of October and our school must start by the first of November. The house would need cleaning, and the children would be ragged and dirty. I had to get home. All these thoughts went through my mind in much less time than it takes to tell them. I decided to go, come what may. "All right, Hi, you stop for me and I'll go." One of the prostitutes had told me one morning what a good, kind boss the madam was. She was so good, she said, to all those girls. Well, she could just be good and kind to me for one night. She could put a cot in the kitchen for me to sleep on. Besides, I thought to myself, no one will harm a woman with a three-weeks-old baby.

Hi stopped for me next morning just at daylight, and I climbed aboard with the expectation of taking a thirty-five-mile ride on top of a load of lumber. It was a dead-X wagon, one without any springs. I also faced the prospect of staying all night in a house of prostitution, but I was headed for home and my babies, and nothing could daunt me. I was feeling very happy and kept singing the old cowboy song— "Going home, going home, where coyotes howl and cattle roam."

I was doing fine for the first ten miles, but then I began to weaken. My shoulders began to slump, and black waves passed before my eyes. I thought sure I was going to faint and wondered if I fell off my high perch on the wagon, if it would kill baby and me. I hung on to the jockey box with all my might. The box is a receptacle built in the middle of a freight wagon to hold small tools, such as monkey wrenches, hammers, and horseshoeing outfits.

Just then an outfit pulled out around us. This was entirely a one-way road, so in meeting or passing, someone had to drive out in the rocks and sagebrush to get around. This fellow was driving a team hitched to a surrey—the old-fashioned kind with the fringe on top—pulling a single-seated top buggy tied on behind. He waved to us to stop. He had a road map spread out on his lap, which showed the forks in the road at the Twenty Mile House. He explained to us that he was a salesman for the Studebaker Carriage Manufacturing Company, and that his company had shipped a load of carriages to Reno. Finding everyone there automobile minded, they had ordered their salesman to hire a team, hooking on all the carriages he could, and drive out into the back country to sell them for anything he could get. I've often wondered at the loss those carriage companies must have taken at the advent of the automobile.

He wanted to know of us which road had the most population. I piped up and said, "The lefthand road." It was really true, for our road had two families living on it in the next thirty miles, and the other road had only one. I asked him if I could ride with him. No matter which road he decided to take, I would have an easy ten-mile ride to the Twenty Mile House, but I made my mind up then to have his mind made up to go my way by the time we reached the forks in the road. I managed it. We trotted right past the house, never stopping, thus missing the only chance I ever had to spend the night in a house of prostitution.

It was late in the evening when we arrived at our place. I began to call "Whoooohoooo" as soon as we turned in at the gate. The children heard my call and, ragged and dirty as I had thought, they all came running down to meet me. But they were all healthy. Daddy had done a good job of taking care of them, and I couldn't complain at a little dirt.

❧[**Eleven**]❧

School was to start November first, and the next two weeks were busy ones for me. There was a good deal of housecleaning to do, besides the making of new little dresses and shirts. Our new teacher arrived, and I had picked another winner. I think someone ought to write an ode to country school teachers. They're in a class by themselves. Ours were always so willing to help on any of my propositions, from helping the neighbors dig potatoes, to helping the children drive the steers to town. No matter how hard the work, they always considered it a lark.

We had no trouble keeping teachers through the year, for one of the cowboys was always there when school let out to take her for a grand gallop through the hills.

In the fall of the year we always had a scourge of wood rats. One big fellow, a forerunner of the rest of the tribe, had arrived early and began to gnaw a hole in our house. He was a bold one, and you could look out in the yard at any time of the day and see him trotting around.

The dogs would have nothing to do with him, for they feared those sharp, protruding teeth. They arched their backs, the ruffs of their necks bristling, but they stayed at a safe distance. For days I had been after Daddy and Edson to kill this rat, for once they come, they're there to stay, and you have to kill them to be rid of them. We'd taken down the screens, and the windows were open day and night. The rat could have come in the window at any time, but he chose to sit on a narrow window ledge above the bedroom window and gnaw a hole through the wall to gain entry.

One night he was exceptionally industrious, and about twelve o'clock I became so annoyed at his gnawing that I couldn't stand it any longer. I decided I could kill that wood rat with the broom. I crept out of bed in my nightgown and bare feet, quietly tiptoeing to the kitchen for the broom. I came back and leaned out the window. Sure enough, as I looked up, there he was, chewing away.

I whammed at him with the broom again and again, but he could dodge the blows with the greatest of ease, never missing a gnaw. Finally with a well aimed stroke, I hit him, knocking him off his perch. He fell across my face as he hurtled down. I screamed in revulsion. Then as I looked down, the animal fairly bounced as he hit and ran back up the wall to his narrow window ledge, going on with his work, as though he had never been interrupted. I struck at him again and again, laughing all the time. At last I was able to connect again with a good hard blow, and this time he fell squarely in my face, and my, how I screamed!

Daddy and Edson had been awakened by all this commotion, and hearing me laughing one moment and screaming the next, they could come to only one conclusion. Now they were at my side, one on the right, the other on the left.

Daddy had been expecting me to collapse mentally or physically from the hard work I was doing, and now he thought my mind was gone for sure. He stood there gently stroking my face saying, "Dear old lady! Poor old lady! Gone at last! Just too much damned hard work."

Edson on the other side of me was shaking me as hard as he could by the shoulders saying, "Talk to us, Ma! Say something. Tell us you're not crazy!"

There I stood between the two of them, laughing so hard I couldn't talk. Between peals of laughter, I'd squeak out, "I'm all right! I'm all right!" But they were so sure I was crazy neither of them would believe me. Finally I straightened up and shoved each one of them away from me. Holding them at arms' length I said, "Now listen to me! I'm not crazy. I'm just having a try at killing that rat that I've been after you fellows to kill for days. Now go on back to bed. I'm all right!"

They both returned to bed, mumbling. I heard Daddy saying, "Well, old lady, you're damn near crazy!" He'd been caught showing a little affection that he didn't like to express, and he was disgusted over it.

Edson was muttering, "Gee whiz, Ma, don't ever do that to us again. Wake us up first, and tell us you're not nuts."

The next day Daddy killed the rat.

That next evening Edson came home from his trap lines with a broad grin on his face. "Well, Ma, we're even now," he told me. He had a line of traps strung from Dogskin Mountain down across Warm Springs Flat. A coyote had been caught in one of the sets on Dogskin and had gotten away, dragging the traps after him. Edson had tracked him easily through the rocks and sagebrush, but when he hit the dry brown grass at Warm Springs he lost the track. The grass there has such a springiness to it that the trap dragging over it never made a mark. The coyote and the grass were so much the same color that it was impossible to detect him unless the animal was moving.

Edson circled all around the flat, but could find no place where the coyote had gone out; he was cornered in there some place, but as one brown bump looked like every other, Edson gave up after searching for hours. He decided to have a bath in the hot spring. We had installed a crude bathtub in the water, made of rough lumber with a removable gate at one end of the tub. Often in passing there we stopped for a hot bath. He rode his horse, Nell, to the spring, stripped, and got into the tub.

Then he thought of looking "Indian" as we call it, that is by getting your eye on the level of the object you're looking for. It's surprising how well it works. It did now for him. Sitting there in the sunken bathtub, looking out over the bumpy grass—all the land around the springs is raised up in bumpy little rises—he saw one brown bump moving. He knew it was his coyote. Not having time to dress, for fear he'd lose sight of that slightly moving object, he jumped naked on old Nell, screaming and yelling to keep the coyote moving, and Nell at a dead gallop. He finally drove the coyote out into the sagebrush where it got tangled and he killed it. Tying it on his saddle he went back and finished his bath.

Now he was home grinning at me, and saying, "Now, Ma, we're even. If anyone had seen me bare naked, riding old Nell at a gallop and screaming and hollering, I'd have had a hard time convincing them I wasn't crazy! You can't always just stop and explain that you're all right."

Things went along smoothly all that year, and before we knew it the summer of 1913 was upon us. That summer should go down in Nevada history as the year of the great cloudbursts. There were numerous cloudbursts all over the state. One in Pershing County completely wiped out a little tent town called Seven Troughs, killing two men. Another at the foot of Geiger Grade, where my husband's sister lived, had caused them to rush to the safety of the high hills, where they watched the debris and sagebrush float over the top of their house. We had one just four miles from home in the Milk Ranch Canyon. That one washed away the Mateo Ranch barn with a stallion tied in it.

About this time I had to make a trip to town for supplies. Daddy was very uneasy about my going and made me promise to start home early, as the cloudbursts had all come in the afternoon. I made the trip, bought my supplies, and had them tied down tight with the wagon canvas. That morning I started home way before daylight. I was on the old upper road near Stormy Canyon fifteen miles from town when the black clouds came sailing toward each other from the east and west. I was scared and watching them closely. It surely looked like a cloudburst to me. The clouds were black, the lightning bright, the thunder loud, and then a terrible wind began to blow with cyclone force.

Now I was really frightened. I had a heavy load on the wagon. I stood up with one foot on the dashboard, one foot in the bed of the wagon, and began to scream and hit old Johnny with every step. Then the rain began to pour down, and the wind continued its terrific gale. I heard a terrible roar, which I knew could be nothing but the side of the mountain coming down. I looked back and besides all the roar, wind, and thunder I saw something else to frighten me even more. A perfect wall of water—you could call it nothing else—was bearing down upon me. It was fast coming my way, though it hadn't reached me as yet. I had poor Johnny at a dead gallop, but I kept screaming and striking him with my whip. I was simply out of my mind with fear. Each time I looked back the wall of water seemed nearer to me. I ran the old horse six miles just barely keeping ahead of the advancing storm.

Then we struck Bacon Rind Flat and Johnny's feet went out from under him. I was not over my fright, but I knew we could run no further. Then my sense of humor came uppermost, and I thought of a funny story about a little school boy. His teacher had given him a problem in arithmetic for homework. The problem was this: A cat had fallen into a well. It gave the dimensions of the well. If the cat jumped up two feet and fell back eighteen inches, and so on to the top, how many jumps would it take the cat to get to the top. Little Tommy was working hard but getting his figures reversed. At last his father said, "Come, Tommy. It's bedtime."

Tommy looked up sleepily and said, "Dad, I'd just as well go to bed. If I work any longer here I'll have that cat in hell!"

This was something like my present problem. We were traveling upgrade when Johnny had lost his footing. Now if we made any progress at all it would be backwards toward that storm. And although the roar had stopped the wall of water was still advancing my way. I jumped out of the wagon and helped Johnny up. I had run the poor old fellow nearly to death. He was breathing hard, and his sides were heaving. It was a terrible situation. We were twenty miles from a human being in the midst of the storm. I put my arms around Johnny's neck and pressed my face close to his. I felt sorry to think I'd run him so hard, beating him with the whip. I said, "God forgive me for beating my poor old horse. And forgive me, Johnny, I didn't intend to be so mean." I stood there hugging him, looking the situation over, and talking aloud to Johnny. It was a great comfort to have something alive that I could be close to.

We were out on a broad flat with several miles between us and the hills. It would have to be a regular Noah's Ark flood to do us any harm. I don't know how long I stood there with my arms around Johnny's neck, watching the cloudburst. Miraculously, as I watched, it slowly turned and passed away toward the east, leaving us unharmed, but thoroughly drenched.

I was hours getting across Bacon Rind Flat, so called because it is greasy and slippery when wet. When Johnny would get frightened at all the slipping and sliding I would jump out and go around to his head, put my arms around him, and talk to him, which seemed to calm him. Many times in the two-mile trek across the flat we had to stop and rest. From there on home it was good going. Everyone was anxiously awaiting us when we got home, for there had been a small cloudburst down our own canyon.

On my next trip to town, I saw that the roar had

been, as I thought, a part of the mountain washing down. Boulders, weighing tons, had been bobbled around like corks. Had I been ten minutes later, I wouldn't be telling my story.

⁂| **Twelve** |⁂

We had always depended on Edson's trapping for the greater part of our yearly income. Last year the money had come in handy for the baby and the farm implements. This year I had vowed to buy a horse. It was embarrassing to have to borrow a horse every time I needed one, and though the PF company was very generous and kind about loaning us one it went against my pride.

The price of furs fluctuates more than any commodity on the market. This year it was down, and we could get only a dollar and a half for prime hides. The whole catch wouldn't be worth the price of a horse. So how was I to get it, I wondered? I still clung to the idea, but it didn't promise to be much else.

One cold November day I was down at the neighboring sheep ranch. The wealthy owner had come out in his big Cadillac. That was before cars were enclosed, and what a cold thing they were to ride in. One had to bundle up well and have lots of robes. He had one robe that especially attracted my attention. It was made out of Coyote hides with the heads cut off and the ends butted together. The tails were left on for trimming. I looked that robe over thoroughly and then asked the sheep man, "Who made this for you?"

He told me that an Indian had tanned the hides and made the robe, and he told me the Indian's name.

I thought, "Well, if an Indian can make a robe like that, I can too." I lost no time in hunting up the Indian. He was kind enough to give me his recipe for tanning and showed me how to cut the hides, using only a ten inch strip from the middle of the back of each fur. Then he showed me how to sew them together. I don't remember the recipe now, but I know I soaked the hides in some kind of strong solution and then let them partially dry; after that it was a case of rubbing and patience. You hold the hides in your hands with the insides together and rub and rub. The more you rub the softer the hide gets. We all joined in the "rubbing bee"—teacher and all. Every night after supper everyone would get a hide and begin rubbing. Sometimes to break the monotony we'd have Edson play a tune on his accordion, which he had bought from a sheepherder for fifteen dollars. It was surprising what a lift the music would give us.

I was in something of a hurry to get the robe made, for I wanted to sell it during the holidays. When the tanning was finished, I sewed the hides together. It was not a pleasant job, for each time I breathed in, I spit the fur out of my mouth in gobs and blew it out of my nostrils, but I kept on till it was put together, and then I lined it with a brand new horse blanket, which I'd payed six dollars for. It was now just two weeks before Christmas, and Daddy was making the trip to town for supplies. We put the robe on display in the window of a harness shop, which the owner had kindly given us permission to do for a commission. I don't know how we arrived at our price, but we decided to ask eighty dollars for it. The shop owner put a price tag on it for a hundred dollars—the difference to be his commission. I thought surely that anyone able to drive a Cadillac would want that robe, but to my great disappointment it didn't sell. It just hung in the window, collecting dust until March.

At that time I made a trip into town to take the teacher in to attend Teachers' Institute. We had to dismiss school for a week so that she could go. Her folks came out after her in their car, and she had invited me to come in and spend the week with them, which gave me a splendid opportunity to sell my robe and buy a horse. As I was leaving, Edson gave me a rousing whack on the back and said, "You can do it, Ma. Of course you can. You can do anything."

The evening we arrived in town I read in the paper that some horses were being sold from a ranch estate that was being settled. I knew the man who had the horses for sale on consignment, and right away I thought, "There's my horse."

Bill Williams had a big corral up on Riverside Drive. He had twenty-five horses corralled and for sale. I rose early the next morning and walked up to see Bill. I no sooner entered the corral when I spied a three-year-old brown Belgian mare. To my notion she was a beauty—just exactly what I wanted. From the very first my eyes were blinded to seeing any other animal. Bill was asking sixty-five dollars for her—I was asking eighty for the robe. I told him about the robe and told him I wanted to trade with him—the robe for the mare, and I wanted fifteen dollars to boot.

We got in his jalopy and went after the robe. Then we dickered and dickered from Sunday morning till the next Saturday night. I was at the corral every day, but not trying to get any other horse.

I would have the trade just about made when Bill's

little eighty-year-old mother would come out and
say, "Now, Bill! Don't you sell that lady the horse."
Bill would usher her back into the house none too
kindly, and we would go on with our horse trading.
The professional horse trader is the hardest man on
earth to deal with—I know. Late Saturday evening I
gave up and traded the robe straight across for the
mare. Then I sat down and cried on the first stairway
I came to on the way back to the house, thinking I'd
been beaten out of fifteen dollars. When we had at
last made the deal, his little, old mother came out, put
her arms around my neck and said, "I've tried so
hard to keep Bill from selling you that horse. It's the
meanest thing that ever came into the corral! Now
that the sale is made, I'm asking God to bless her and
make her a good horse for you." Her blessing must
have worked, for there never was a truer, better
horse. She was unbroken at the time, but some
friends of ours who lived near Reno wanted an extra
horse to do their spring plowing, and I made arrangements with them to use my colt. They plowed
with her for a month, and she was thoroughly broken.

Daddy went to town, bought a new harness and a
tongue for the spring wagon, hitched the colt up with
Johnny, and proudly drove the two horses home.

That same summer I acquired a saddle horse in a
most unexpected way. I had driven into town, and
while I was there I heard of a man who wanted to buy
our old transfer wagon that we had stored in Reno.
This man, Mr. Murrey, ran a dairy and hog ranch,
and he wanted the transfer wagon to haul slops for
the hogs. I drove up to see him. Just as I pulled into
his yard, he was hitching up his team to his milk

delivery wagon. One of the horses was balking, and he was standing in the wagon beating the horse with the butt end of the buggy whip and swearing till the very air turned blue.

As he saw me, he halted his whip in midair, fairly glaring at me. I guess no one likes to be seen beating a dumb animal. I called out, "Mister, would you like to sell her?" I already had planned a trade in the back of my mind.

He swore. "If you'll take the blankety-blank old bitch, I'll give her to you."

"No," I told him, "I don't want you to give her to me, but I heard you wanted to buy an old transfer wagon that we own. I'll trade you the wagon for her."

"Take her, lady, take her! I'll even throw in the head stall and halter rope." He unhitched her and tied her on behind my wagon, stopping long enough to make out a bill of sale for the horse, while I made out one for the wagon. I drove away feeling I had made a wonderful trade. The horse was a brown thoroughbred mare, and I could visualize a long string of beautiful colts from our mare and a Morgan stallion that the PF company owned. I knew I could get the cowboys to breed her for me for nothing.

After I got half a mile from Murrey's dairy ranch, I got out of the wagon and went back to pet and get acquainted with my new animal. Her name was Kate. She had a lovely brown coat, but there were great, cruel welts all over her hips. I petted her and stroked her, promising that she'd get no more beatings. I knew she balked, but we didn't intend to drive her. She was to be just a saddle horse and brood mare.

She was heavy with foal when I got her—she had

been bred to a jack, and she brought us a mule colt. We called him Rastus, and nobody loved Rastus, for he kicked from the day he was born. We never had a fence he couldn't jump, nor a rope he couldn't break. Rastus was the only animal that ever came on our place that wasn't loved. Lord, how I hated that mule!

He followed his mother wherever we rode her, and when we were herding cattle, it seemed to be his great delight to jump in the middle of them, and start braying and kicking. Once when Rastus was about three years old I had occasion to ride Kate into Reno. We tied Rastus to the manger in the corral with an inch rope. I gave the children orders to feed and water him while I was gone, but by no means to let him out. When I was about halfway to town, I heard hee-haw, hee-haw. Here came Rastus, his head held to one side to keep from stepping on the rope, coming at a high lope and braying every step. He had chewed the rope in two. Now I had a problem! What would I do with the loose mule? I couldn't take him through town running loose, for he might kick half a dozen children on the way. I sat on Kate and puzzled. What will I do? That big question was always coming up in my life.

I knew a rancher half a mile out of Sparks, so I decided to go in that way and ask him to take care of the mule for me. When I rode in to his corral, he was sitting on the bench whittling. He looked up and said, "Where did you get that beautiful mule?"

"Raised him. Want to buy him?"

"Nope. I don't want to buy him myself, but I know a fellow who does. He's had me looking out for some time for a mule to match one of his. This will be a pretty good match, and it's the finest mule I've ever seen."

So we made arrangements for him to sell Rastus for me. "You sell him for whatever you can," I told him, "Take your commission out and give me the rest, and I'll be satisfied. In the meantime put the mule and my mare in your barn while I go into town."

I walked the half mile to Sparks and caught the streetcar into Reno. When my business was finished three days later, I went back to get Kate. My friend had sold the mule, and he counted out seventy-five dollars for me. I never knew or cared what his commission was. I guess there was nothing wrong with the mule, for he was a beautiful animal. There was just something wrong with us—we didn't understand mules. I was never so proud and happy over any other sale I ever made.

Kate was a wonderful success as a brood mare, and our long string of colts materialized, but she was never a howling success as a saddle animal. It was fun to ride her along the trap line. If there was something in the trap, she would sense it several hundred yards away and plainly demonstrate what tales a horse's ears can tell. She would tell me as plain as any langauge if I had something in my traps. I couldn't get her within a hundred yards of a trapped animal. When the animal was dead she made no fuss about having it tied on her saddle, but she was afraid of a trapped wild animal.

She had been raised in the Truckee Meadows where the traveling was smooth, and it was her nature to run, for it had been bred in her for generations. Out here she constantly encountered rocks and sagebrush, things she was entirely unfamiliar with. It's strange to note the difference between a hill-raised horse and a valley-raised horse. One that had been raised among the rocks can run through them at top speed, but old Kate often stumbled and fell. When the sagebrush tickled her belly, she would jump straight into the air and simply go wild.

One day while Edson was riding her on the mountain, he fell in with an Indian who was running wild horses. He took out after them on Kate. He came to a blind canyon where the rim rocks dropped abruptly. The trail ran around the head of the rim rocks, but Kate was determined to go straight across. Edson couldn't guide her, and as she went over the sheer drop he jumped to safety. She fell about twenty feet, cutting her whole chest open. Edson and the Indian had to go two miles down the canyon and then back up to where she hung to rescue her. They led her down to the Hardscrabble Ranch, where the Indian lived. Next day Edson borrowed a horse from his friend and came home. He and I were talking it over quietly, trying to keep Daddy from hearing, for he was bedfast at the time and we didn't want to upset him. But just try to keep something that you don't want known from ears that want to hear. A.J. heard us all right, and called out, "If the kid's all right, then to hell with the horse! Take the gun over and shoot her."

We went into Daddy's bedroom to talk it over and decided that if Kate wasn't able to walk home, Edson was to shoot her. Edson took a saddle horse of his own, leading the Indian's horse back. The next day Kate was able to walk home—the worst cut up animal, still alive, that I have ever seen. She'd fallen on sharp rocks, making a jagged tear, and exposing the great, white breast bones.

I decided to fix her. First I put a twitch around her

upper lip. A twitch is made of a piece of baling wire fastened onto a stick. You wrap the line around the horse's upper lip and have someone hold the stick. If the animal stands very still the twitch is not painful, but if there's the least pull on it it hurts the sensitive lip. Alice dearly loved horses, so she asked to help me by holding the twitch. As I went to work on the wound, the first little jerk Kate made, Alice fainted. We had to stop the operation and get her out of the corral. Then I went on alone. I had a large fountain syringe of the kind they use on horses. I filled it with boiled water that was disinfected with carbolic acid, tied the syringe to a post, and using the spray I washed out all the sand and gravel from the wound. Then I took a sterilized needle and white silk thread and sewed up the ragged edges of the skin. I dressed it every other day for weeks, and it healed rapidly. When it was completely well, there was never the sign of a scar on her beautiful satiny coat. I was surely proud of my second operation. The saddle that had gone over the bluff with Kate was almost a complete loss. We salvaged nothing from it but the stirrups and latigo.

⁍[**Thirteen**]⁌

In making my coyote robe I had used only the best fur, leaving the flank and belly fur, which to me looked too good to throw away. I thought, "Why can't I dye that fur and make something out of it?"

I had some Diamond dye for wool, which I dissolved and put into a boiler of water until I had the desired color; then I put in the skins and boiled them in the dyebath, when all at once I discovered I had a slimy mess of coyote hair and shredded hide. It made me sick at my stomach to even empty it into the hole I had prepared to bury it in.

In my homesteading experience I had achieved many accomplishments, but now I was sure I couldn't dye fur.

We were gaining some. We had a saddle horse as well as a good team of work horses with which to do our summer's work. Then Daddy took sick again. For weeks he sat propped up in bed, and there seemed to be something worse than shortage of breath ailing him this time.

The cowboys came over and helped me get Daddy to bed in the wagon. Then they drove him to the hospital in Reno. I gave them some money to buy a bill of grub to bring back with them for me. They arrived back next night at midnight, but a cowboy never goes to town without getting drunk, and they were still mighty happy when they reached my place. They were hungry, for they had had nothing to eat since breakfast and the liquor was beginning to wear off.

I invited them in, but at first they were reluctant to come, saying, "Oh, Mom, we're drunk. You ought to kick us out."

"Well, drunk or not, you look like a couple of angels to me, so come in and we'll have a good supper." I made a big pan of biscuits, coffee, and fried some ham and eggs.

They had made a special trip to get Daddy to the hospital, and had brought back my supplies, so why should I care if they were a little drunk?

Edson had gone to work for the PF outfit in the hayfields that year on the first of June, and he worked through to September, getting a man's wages of a dollar and a half a day. They wound up the haying at the Constantia Ranch one day at noon and were sending the wagons the next day down to the Winnemucca Ranch. Edson, knowing Daddy was in the hospital and that we would need money, was so anxious to get home, he walked the whole eighteen miles that afternoon instead of waiting until the next day when he could have ridden home in the wagon.

I must have had a premonition that he was coming, for at dusk I left the children alone and walked across the trail where I met him. We sat down on a rock, and he emptied out his pockets, counting out nearly two hundred dollars in gold and silver. He wanted to know if that would be enough money to get Daddy home, for he seemed to have an idea that we couldn't get Daddy out of the hospital until the bill was paid.

Next morning he hitched up the team and drove proudly in after his father. He paid the hospital bill and had enough money left to buy himself a suit of clothes.

In coming home, as they passed Goshie's, the old fellow came out to see A.J. Next time I rode down that way Goshie asked, "How's the old man?"

"Pretty good, Goshie. Pretty good. He's all well now."

"Good?" said Goshie. "No good! He no good for nothing no more. Better off dead. Never no good no more!"

True, Daddy had looked as if he'd never be up and around again, and Goshie had expressed his opinion in his honest way.

While Daddy was still in the hospital and Edson was away working, our hay had to be harvested. I was so proud to have a team and all the necessary implements that I wasn't thinking about all the hard work involved in putting up the hay. I had ten-year-old Alice to help me in the hayfield, while twelve-year-old Jessie did the cooking and housework. I had cut a few acres down in the lower meadow and was loading it on the wagon when the cowboy boss rode through. He stopped and said, "Mrs. Olds, that looks like an awful hard job for a lady."

"Well, it isn't so hard, but it's slow, and I'm afraid I'll lose some of it before I get it all stacked."

"There's a whole crew of white men at the Winnemucca Ranch," he told me, "and they don't work Sundays. I know every man on the job will give you next Sunday's work. You quit hauling. Get all the rest of your hay cut, raked, shocked, and ready to haul, and I'll guarantee that these men will come over and haul and stack it for you. I'll come with them. You get us a big chicken dinner with strawberry shortcake and whip cream, and that'll be our pay."

Sunday morning here they came. Twelve wagons and twenty-five men. I had only twenty loads of hay, and they had it all stacked and tied down in an hour and a half. Then they sat around waiting in the shade of the cabin for their chicken dinner. That was the only hay ever put up on our homestead that I didn't stack myself. The stack I didn't build is the one that makes the story.

Dear old Goshie—what an honest, good fellow he was. A tried and true friend, as the following experience will show.

The next spring I took down with tick fever, a disease caused by the bite of a sheep-infected wood tick. It's a sickness only sheepherders are supposed to have, but I managed to get it. Until that time I'd never spent a day in bed in my life except in childbirth. No one realized how sick I was—least of all myself. I was delirious with the fever and so happy I didn't notice the pain. I'd been in bed about ten days when Goshie heard about it and came up to see me.

School being out, I was sleeping in the schoolroom away from the noise of the children. Daddy brought Goshie in there to see me. He drew up a chair close to my bed and sat down.

I was almost past talking, so he just sat there and looked at me for some time. After awhile he stooped over me, and ran his hands over my face. I was just beginning to break out in red bumps the size of a pea all over my body. There was no rash—just the painful bumps.

"Ahhhh," he said. "Tick fever. You got tick fever,

sure. Nothing else look like. Come red bumps every place. Hurt like hell. More better you go hospital."

I shook my head.

He insisted. "Yes! You go. You no go—you die sure! You all same sheepherder. He come sick, tick fever. Camp tender come see—like take him to doctor. He no go. Next time camp tender come—sheepherder dead. All same you. No go hospital, you die sure. You no got money?"

I shook my head again. "No, Goshie. No money."

"I givey you plenty." With that he reached in his overalls pocket and brought out six twenty-dollar gold pieces, pressing them into my hand. "You needa more money, I givey you plenty more. My boss, he come today. You make li'l Alice make letter—your sister in Reno. I givey letter my boss. He take back to town—your sister."

Fortunately the plan succeeded. My sister-in-law was out to the ranch in her Model-T Ford the same day. Our sagebrush telegraph had worked fast. She had driven out through a snowstorm although it was the first of May. Cars in those days were not equipped with windshield wipers, and she had to stop every few minutes to wipe off the snow so she could see to drive. As it was storming so badly, we decided that she should stay all night. That delay was almost the death of me, for a blood clot settled in my leg during the night, and by morning the leg was almost the size and color of a stove pipe. Tick fever was, at that time, ninety percent fatal, without the added complications of a blood clot.

Next morning the skies were clear, and the snow had nearly all melted. We started early, leaving behind some lonesome-looking crying children. They all thought I was never coming back, and Daddy thought so most of all. We'd been planting potatoes when I got sick, and he didn't even bring down the unplanted sack of seed, but let it lie up there and freeze in our late spring storm. Later, when I asked him why he didn't finish planting the potatoes, he replied, "Hell, old lady. I thought you weren't coming back, and if you didn't we weren't going to need any potatoes." I don't know what he had intended to do.

Miraculously, I recovered.

Goshie's six twenties, with a little more added, cleared my doctor and hospital bills. It was years before we were able to repay him—not until after World War I when we had gone off gold standard. Until that time Nevada had used only gold and silver and a greenback was an oddity. When I finally got enough money to pay Goshie I was so proud of myself that I was aghast when I saw the look of disgust on his face when I offered him the money.

He spread the bills out in his fingers saying, "No good. That kind of money no good. No can bury that kind." He had never had a bank account, preferring to bury his money. "Me want gold," he insisted. "You go bank. Government got plenty gold." I simply could not make him understand that all the country's gold was locked up in a vault. He just kept looking at those paper bills and saying, "No good! No good for nothing." Then looking straight at me and holding the bills out in his hand he said, "No good for nothing. Wipey ass, that's all." And from the look of disgust on his kind, old face I knew that's what he really thought. Finally though, he stuck the bills in his pocket.

Trouble and hard luck never seems to come singly. I had the tick fever in May. Then in October, Edson, our main support, developed a mastoid condition. We sent him to the hospital in San Francisco to be operated on. We were terribly worried over his condition as well as where we would get the money to live on that fall without his trapping income.

There would be two hundred #3 steel traps lying idle. His father and I discussed with him what we could do about the trapping before we saw him off on the train. I had often ridden with him around the traplines—always turning my back while he killed whatever had been caught.

He had told me, "Watch me, Ma. Don't shoot the animal. All you have to do is hit them a tap with the stick on that bump on their head. That knocks them out. Then pick up one free foot, stretch them out tight, step on their gully-gully [throat] and give them a little kick over the heart. There, it's all done in a second. No bullet holes to spoil the hide." We put Edson on the train and sat there with him before it pulled out. He turned and said to me, "You can run that trapline, Ma. You've seen me do it lots of times." Then, putting his hot feverish hand over mine, he said, "You can do it, Ma. You can do anything." When a child has that much faith in you, you have to try to make good. I promised that I would run the traplines and do the best I could. Bidding him a brave but almost heartbreaking good-bye, and after pinning our address on his coat and putting a copy of it in his purse, we left him with instructions to have the doctor send us a telegram as soon as the operation was over. We drove sadly home.

Next day we received our news from the hospital.

It came in a roundabout way. The telegraph office was at Omira, California, on the Western Pacific Railway, two miles from our Constantia postoffice, which was eighteen miles from our place. As everyone knew everyone else far and near, the telegraph operator knew us. He phoned the message to the postmaster at Constantia. It was given to a cowboy, who rode eighteen miles to deliver it to us. He was an especially tender-hearted cowboy—though I don't believe there are any other kind. It was bad news that he was carrying, and he kept thinking on the way over, "I can't give those folks this message. Maybe Edson isn't as bad off as they think." The nearer he got to our place, the worse he hated to give us the message.

When he finally arrived he told us we had a telegram from the San Francisco hospital, and that Edson was feeling pretty good. Edson did recover and was soon home.

Two years later he was riding with the same cowboy on a mountain ridge in a storm. The cowboy reached in his inside pocket for a dry cigarette paper and pulled out the two-year-old telegram. Handing it to Edson, he said, "Give that to your mother. It won't bother her now. I just couldn't deliver that message two years ago. I felt in my bones that you'd be all right." The telegram red, "Edson dying. Come at once." What a happy thing for us that cowboy changed the message.

While Edson was gone I had to make good my promise to keep up the traplines. Daddy had volunteered to skin the animals—"if you catch any." I know he considered it unlikely. I had watched Edson setting the traps many times, but it's one thing to

watch, and another to really do the trick. I caught my
fingers often in the cruel jaws of those steel traps.
They weren't quite strong enough to break the bones,
but they caused me a good deal of pain. I always
caught my right hand, for the left wasn't strong
enough to open the springs on the trap. To release
my hand, I had to step on the trap with both feet,
raising myself about three inches off the ground. In
this unsteady position I often tipped forward on my
face with my trapped hand back under me, causing
all the more pain in my poor fingers. After many such
an experience, I learned to keep my hand under the
jaws of the trap while setting it.

On my first trip around the trapline I caught a
bobcat. I hadn't expected to catch anything, and now
I was faced with the task of killing what I had caught.

I had never shot a gun in my life. What in the world
would I do? I'm not a natural killer, and I was afraid
to try Edson's method. For awhile I stood there and
bawled good and loud. I had brought along a little .22
Winchester rifle. The magazine held five shells with
which to kill whatever I hoped I wouldn't catch. I
now took careful aim and shot. Nothing happened.
That cat lay there, never blinking an eye. I shot three
times more with no better result. With my one shell
left, I must hit it this time. I drew a little closer, took
careful aim and—BANG. The cat jumped into the air
the full length of the trap chain, letting out a yowl
that frightened me nearly to death.

I dropped my gun and ran down the canyon as fast
as I could go. After running a hundred yards or so, I
came to my senses and realized I must have killed
that cat. I turned and went back to get my gun.
Cautiously I approached the spot where the cat lay.

Sure enough he was dead. I took him out of the trap, made a reset, then with the animal tied on the back of my saddle, I proudly rode home, knowing Daddy would be very surprised at my catch.

He met me at the gate with, "Well, old lady. Caught a cat, huh? How many times did you have to shoot it?"

I didn't want him to know how many times I had shot *at* it, so I said airily, "Just once."

He took the cat out to the shed to skin it, while I went into the house to wash up and prepare supper. A pelt is turned inside out as you skin it, and any mark on the hide will show clearly on the inside. Daddy soon came in, his face simply beaming. He held up the cat hide and said, "Well, old lady. That one bullet made a good many holes in your cat skin." There was the mute evidence. There were ten holes! Each bullet had gone clear through that cat's body.

I was amazed at the fortitude of the cat. He had lain there never batting an eye while four bullets were pumped into him. The last one had evidently gone through his heart. The pelt wasn't much good, but as a miner would say, I had struck pay dirt. Surely shooting and killing would come easier with practice.

On my next trip around I caught a skunk—a beautiful little animal. No wonder the skunk is called "Little Flower" by Walt Disney! He sat there blinking his snappy black eyes with his one foot caught in the cruel trap. My how I cried! I tried to think of some way to get it out of the trap without killing it, but I could think of no way. I circled around behind a big, black sagebrush. (Why I thought a sagebrush would be any protection from a skunk I don't know, but that's what I did.) I balanced my gun carefully on a branch of the bush, took good aim, then squeezed my eyes tight and pulled the trigger. I always closed my eyes when shooting, and anything I hit was purely accidental. I fired all five shells before I opened my eyes. I had hit him a time or two, but the poor little devil was still alive. I cried some more and then picked up a club and waded in to kill him. A club was much more effective in my hands than a gun. The skunk only shot at me once, but his aim was better than mine! My family could hardly live in the same house with me for a month.

My next catch was a bobcat, no more than six weeks old. He was so pretty and appealing that I thought, "Well, I'll take you out of the trap and take you home for a pet." But as I approached him, he sprang at me so viciously, teeth and claws bared ready to tear me to pieces, that I swung on him with my club. (By this time I was carrying a club made from an old broomstick with a hole bored through one end to which I attached a leather thong so I could hang it over my saddle horn, and it would be handy if I needed it.)

On another trip I caught an American eagle. Feeling very patriotic I thought, "Well, I won't kill you." I had read of their vicious beak and claws, so to guard myself from injury I got a forked stick, pinned his head down with it, and got a good hold on his wings right up next to his body. Then I reached my foot out to spring the trap and release his foot. When he felt his trapped foot released, he swung his body toward me with such a force that it nearly knocked me over. Then he stuck the talons of his good foot into my leg right through my clothing. I had to wring his neck to loosen his hold. I had lost my patriotic sympathy for him at that bit of viciousness.

I trapped on all fall catching a hundred and fifty dollars worth of pelts. It was not a great deal compared to what Edson would have brought in, but I was never so proud of any money I had ever made. The pelts were in good shape, for I had learned through bitter experience to kill them Edson's way, by stepping on their gully-gully and kicking them over the heart.

The first one I killed that way was a sad experience. I hit the coyote on top of the head with my club, then while he was senseless I stretched him out, holding to his hind foot. I placed one foot on his throat, and with my other I kicked and kicked. He wouldn't stop breathing. I guess I didn't press down hard enough. I stood there crying and kicking for well onto an hour, but that coyote would not die! I didn't dare let go, but at last he gave up the ghost. Later, with more practice, I could kill them in an instant. And when Edson heard of my trapping success he gave me one of his smacks on the shoulder, saying, "Ma, I knew you could do it." His faith in me had put me to another test.

When Edson was well on the road to recovery, the hospital in San Francisco released him to the care of our Reno specialist. The poor kid was so homesick that he persuaded the doctor to let him come home while there was a three inch cavity running up in back of his ear. He told the doctor, "Ma can dress my wound. I know she can." So the doctor gave him the equipment and instructions for dressing and warned him, "Don't let the wound heal up from the outside. Dress it thoroughly every day."

It was healing rapidly, for each time I dressed it, it took less and less gauze to fill the cavity. Then one morning when I looked at it, it was completely healed over. I was frightened and very worried. Had I let it heal too soon? We were so concerned we made Edson ride into Reno to have the doctor look at it. The doctor said it had healed perfectly, and I had done a wonderful job.

At this time the children were printing a school journal that they called *The Tule Mountain Record*. Every bit of news in the neighborhood got into the school paper. The first installment after Edson's ride to town to have his head examined carried this notice in the Lost & Found column: Lost: A hole in Edson Olds head. Finders please keep it. We don't want it back.

Fourteen

Edson was very fastidious about caring for his furs. One morning he came in from his trapline with two coyotes. He skinned them, but he didn't have enough time to flush and stretch them before school.

Daddy said, "Leave them, and I'll take care of them for you." Edson didn't think Daddy was careful enough with the furs, but just then the school bell rang, so he turned them over to Daddy with a last precaution, "Be careful!"

In stretching the skins, Daddy pulled off one of the tails, and not knowing what else to do with it, he threw it away. When Edson came out of school at recess, he ran around to look at his hides. He came in the house fairly storming at his father, "You've ruined one of the hides. The tail's gone!"

Then I, the peacemaker, came to the rescue. "Where is the tail," I asked. "I'll sew it on, and hide the stitches so they'll never show." Edson brought me the tail and went back to school pacified knowing Ma could fix it.

I sewed the tail on as best I could, but it didn't look right. Something was surely wrong. I knew I had hidden my stitches carefully I thought, "Well, I've done the best I can. I'll just forget it."

When Edson came out of school at noon he went

around to inspect my handiwork. He came in with a broad grin on his face and said, "You did a pretty good job, Ma. Your stitches don't show." Then laughing outright he said, "You sewed the tail on the belly instead of on the back." Well, no wonder it didn't look right. I then went out and sewed the tail where it belonged, and peace was restored.

After we had acquired the desert claim everything looked brighter for us. We were slowly but surely gaining. Our herd of cattle and horses was increasing, and we had a Model-T Ford. I went into chicken ranching in a modest way, and also raised turkeys and geese for the market.

One spring a turkey and a goose both laid eggs in the same nest in an A shaped coop. The goose went to setting first and didn't leave the nest for days. I wanted to rescue the turkey eggs so they wouldn't spoil, but as a setting goose is a rather ferocious bird to disturb I bided my time till the goose would leave the nest to feed.

All the while a goose sets on the nest, the gander stands guard, making a formidable pair to disturb. Finally I saw the goose come off to feed, the gander still standing guard at the front of the coop. I called to Daddy to come with me and stand at the front of the coop to attract the gander's attention, while I got down on my hands and knees at the back of the coop to reach under and rescue the turkey eggs. But the old goose saw us and promptly came running back and got on her nest. As I reached in to get the eggs, she bit my hand unmercifully, then the gander came around to the back of the coop and bit and flogged me from behind. I took an awful punishment for a few minutes, but succeeded in getting the turkey eggs.

I looked up and there stood Daddy at the front of

the coop laughing. "Well, old lady," he exclaimed, "I wasn't a hell of an attraction, was I?"

That spring, after a heavy winter, Warm Springs Creek, which was usually a dry wash on the desert, became a raging torrent. Some bartenders from Reno, while driving through the desert, saw this big stream of water and thinking the stream was always that heavy, they went in together and homesteaded one hundred and sixty acres of land apiece. They built a big reservoir, dug a ditch from the creek to the reservoir (both were in sandy soil), and then they broke out and planted ten acres in alfalfa and wheat. They built a five-foot chicken-wire fence around their crop to keep out the jack rabbits, and they built a one-room cabin. Then they sent out an old opiate addict to irrigate for them and keep the water flowing through the ditch.

We called the old fellow "Goofy Frank," and the bartenders' homestead was referred to as the "Goofy Camp." It was never a success, for the first time the water was turned into the sandy ditch the banks caved in, and the water never reached the reservoir. "Goofy Frank" tried his best to repair the breaks in the ditch, but he would no sooner get one place fixed when another would cave in. The odds were too much against him. The bartenders gave up after the first summer, and after spending thousands of dollars they deserted the place. The name of the place was changed from "Goofy Camp" to "The Bartenders' Dream."

Later, we bought all they had to sell on their place, which amounted to the cabin and the chicken wire around the ten acres of land.

I had an amusing experience in buying "The Bartenders' Dream." It was during prohibition days, and the bartenders had gone into moonshining. They had their still up on an almost inaccessible place on Mount Rose. We had learned through the sagebrush telegraph where they were located. One of them had written me that they would sell the house and wire for one hundred dollars. We needed both. Edson went with me in our Model-T Ford. We had some difficulty locating their cabin and still among the thick pine timber on Mount Rose, but we finally spotted it.

As we neared the cabin we saw three men come out and take out across the timber at a dead run. Knowing they had mistaken us for prohibition officers we stepped on the gas and called their names. Hearing us they turned and came back, looking rather foolish, and the deal was quickly made. We had bought out another homesteader.

About 1914 eastern divorcees, or dudes, as we called them, began to invade our outlying country buying land. Hi sold out to one of them, moved his horses into Reno, and started one of our first riding academies in town. When I told old Goshie of Hi's new enterprise, he shrugged his shoulders, saying, "Pretty good! Hi make good in riding stable. He know plenty about horses. He make it nice to the ladies. Sure. He make good."

The woman that Hi sold out to was a flighty divorcee. We had great fun watching the happenings up at the widow's that summer. First she drove out in her new Cadillac with her ten-year-old girl and twelve canary birds in twelve different cages. Next she added a milk cow and a few chickens. On another trip to town she bought two hundred head of fine young cows, and hiring some cowboys to help her, she drove them up on Tule Mountain where there were thousands of acres of good grazing land. And on her *next* trip to town she got married to a straggly, bony-looking old gent. His name was Skaggs, and it fitted him exactly. We called him Old Skaggs from the beginning. In a week's time they had a quarrel, and she took the child and the Cadillac, and away she went to town. Soon after she left, Old Skaggs hitched up the team and spring wagon and followed her, stopping first at our place to ask me to go up and do the chores while they were away. I said I would. I didn't mind feeding the chickens and milking the cow, but Oh! Those canary birds!

I'd always felt sorry for a bird in a cage, and now I was afraid I'd forget to do everything that needed to be done for them. When Mrs. Skaggs was there she took great care of them, moving them around to sun and shade as need be. I didn't have much time to care for birds, so I pulled the big table out in the middle of the floor and placed all twelve cages on the table. Then I carefully fed and watered the canaries each day.

The newlyweds soon made up and were back home in a few days. In a week or two the same performance was repeated, and back I went to do their chores. The third time it happened Mrs. Skaggs took Old Skaggs in the Cadillac with her. As they both had a Nevada residence, they could get a divorce as easy as buying a bill of grub. That time she did get a divorce, and we saw no more of Old Skaggs.

The widow, by this time disgusted with the whole country, sold her cattle. The buyer brought out a bunch of horses and some cowboys, and they rounded up the cattle on Tule Mountain and drove them to town—all but four head, which they couldn't find.

The Merry Widow stopped at our place and sold the remaining four head to me—that is, she'd sell them if I could find them. Daddy didn't want me to buy the cattle. "Why in hell," he asked, "didn't you tell her you didn't have the money to pay for them?"

I did tell her that, but I also told her that we would have the money by September when I sold our little herd of steers. I wasn't to pay her for the cows until I found them and had them in my possession. It was a good deal. One of the cows proved to be a wonderful milk cow. We called her Old Skaggs.

We had no use for another milk cow, but we had a neighbor three miles away who had a wife and three children, but no milk cow. We loaned him Old Skaggs, and the children drove her over to the homesteader's land. He was to raise the calf for us, and have the cow bred. Then when she went dry our children would go over and drive the cow and calf home. The next spring we would do the same thing over again.

We drove Old Skaggs back and forth for three years. One time while taking her over to the neighbor, Alice rode ahead leading the cow, and Jessie was riding behind herding. About half way there, Alice had a call from nature and taking the dallies around the saddle horn, she dismounted.

When she pulled her riding pants down Old Skaggs got frightened and plunged ahead toward Alice's horse, wrapping the rope around Alice's feet. There was Alice strung out in mid-air between the horse and cow, with her pants down and her bare bottom scraping along the gravelly road. How she escaped without severe injury is a mystery.

When the girls returned home that evening Alice

drew a picture of the whole performance. She always illustrated her stories with pictures, and how I wish I had saved them.

In the third year the homesteader bought Old Skaggs and kept her three years more. When he sold his place and moved away, he sold the cow to another homesteader over in Redrock Valley, who owned her for four years.

Then a hard winter came, and having no hay, he advertised his stock for sale. I drove over in the Ford and bought the cows—eleven of them including Old Skaggs. The cows were very poor and had to be moved immediately. The homestead was twenty-five miles from our place across Dogskin Valley.

I planned to go over the next day on horseback and bring them home. Next morning Edson and I started out at two A.M., for we had a fifty-mile ride ahead of us. We arrived at the Redrock Homestead about ten A.M. After resting awhile we turned the cattle out and headed home.

From the very first Old Skaggs took the lead. She traveled along the fence with her head down sniffing the ground. When she reached the end of the homesteader's fence she pointed her nose toward Tule Mountain and made a bee line for home with the other cows and Edson and I following her lively gait. When we turned them in our meadow gate, she broke into a dead run and headed for the corral. She hadn't been home for seven years. Such was an old cow's memory.

We had often heard of dogs and horses traveling great distances to reach home, but that was the first demonstration I had ever had of an old cow's homing instinct.

Fifteen

Mrs. Skaggs, the "Merry Widow," was our first encounter with a dude. After her, many more followed. They were impressed with our cowboys, thinking them very romantic. They were a different type of man from what the eastern women had been used to. Many of them married the cowboys—the dude, usually quite well off, furnished the wherewithal to live on, and the cowboy furnished the romance.

Very few of these marriages were ever a success, for the new wife would try immediately to change her husband into an eastern gentleman, even going so far as to make him wear tails for dinner. I could never understand why a woman would marry one type of man, and then try to make him into something completely different.

Goshie's predictions about Hi were right. Hi did make "plenty money" in his riding stable. Then the inevitable happened. A wealthy divorcee fell in love with him, and they were soon married. She bought him one of the PF company's ranches on the eastern side of Tule Mountain, overlooking Pyramid Lake. They built a thirteen room ranch house with three bathrooms, and of course, Hi dressed in tails for dinner. They lived a drunken and hilarious life for a few short years. Then one morning they found dear old Hi dead in his chair.

Sometime before, he had made known his wishes to be cremated and have his ashes scattered around the monument on Tule Mountain overlooking his old homestead. In Hi's brief access to wealth, he had never forgotten his cowboy friends, so now his widow, May, wanted to continue in their good esteem. She made quite a fete out of the funeral ceremony of scattering the ashes.

Every cowboy in the country around was there on horseback, as that was their only means of transportation. It was six miles up a steep tortuous trail from the ranch to the top of the mountain. We must have made a queer looking procession going up that trail. The ashes had arrived by mail from Sacramento where the body had been shipped for cremation. First in the funeral procession was an old-timer of a cowboy named Johnny, a very good friend of Hi's.

He carried the ashes and led Hi's saddled, bridled, and riderless horse with Hi's beautifully tooled leather boots hanging backwards on either side of the saddle. Then came the tipsy widow, and while it was yet only ten A.M., she had already imbibed too freely. Then came the rest of the mourners and the near relations followed by a motley crowd of cowboys, sportsmen from Reno, neighbors, and friends.

As we passed through the ranch gate, one of the cowboys, who was a little tipsy, took it into his head to give Hi a farewell salute, and fired his gun several times into the air. This frightened Hi's riderless horse, which began to buck and tear around. While he was bucking, he managed to get the lead rope under the tail of Johnny's horse, which also began to buck, nearly unseating old Johnny, who was trying to calm his horse, keep a tight hold on the ashes and the lead rope, and at the same time trying to stay in his saddle. With the two horses carrying on, the empty boots on Hi's saddle flapping in the air, the antics poor Johnny was going through, and the cowboys kiyiing in the background, yelling, "Stay with him, Johnny! Stay with him!" it was a hilarious scene for several minutes.

Eventually they were able to calm the horses, and we wound our way slowly up the mountain. Arriving at the monument, May and Johnny dismounted and walked slowly round and round the big rock pile. Everyone began to sing "When It's Round Up Time In Texas," only we changed the words a little:

> When it's round up time on Tule
> And the bloom is on the sage.

We all intoned it mournfully. As a strange coincidence, the yellow sagebrush that blooms in the fall was in full flower. Round and round we rode, following May and Johnny, singing cowboy songs all the while.

As we marched, May was trying valiantly to scatter the ashes, but she seemed to be having difficulty. Evidently the crematorium had not done a good job on cooking Hi, and soon she became exasperated. Stopping, she handed the box to Johnny and said loud enough for us all to hear, "Here, see if you can get the damn stuff out of there."

It was no easier for Johnny to remove the ashes and bones, for they were bones, and are bones, lying there to this day—finger bones, toe bones, and teeth! After forty years, they can still be found.

While Johnny was in the process of scattering the ashes, we all went gallantly on singing cowboy songs. It was a funeral long to be remembered in our part of the country.

Usually when a man's ashes are scattered, that's the end. But May wanted to do a little bit more for Hi. She had a silver plaque made with his name engraved on it and placed it at the foot of the monument, intending to have it cemented on. She never got around to doing it.

A sheepherder, coming on the plaque, stole it, thinking he could get some money for it. Finding it had no commercial value, he brought it back. Two years later, while riding on the mountain one day, I found it lying several hundred yards away from the monument. I picked it up and placed it at the base where it had originally been placed. On my next trip I took along some cement and fastened it securely to the monument.

May didn't have long to grieve over Hi, for in a very short time she drank herself to death. Her body was shipped east and was accompanied to the depot by only one attendant, for we all felt she had been the cause of our beloved Hi's untimely death.

There was only one dude and cowboy marriage that I know of that was a success. A very dear cowboy friend of ours fell in love with a dude from Chicago and soon married her. I think the success of that match lay in the fact that the cowboy refused to change his way of living. He always said, "By God, she married me as a cowboy, and a cowboy I'll remain!" And he wore his Levi's to dinner.

They had a little girl, who miraculously grew to be a talented and accomplished young lady, against great odds. Her father liked to dress her in Levi's, checkered shirts, and big hats. He taught her to swear and use rough language like the cowboys. On the other hand, her mother liked to dress her in puffy-ruffles and take her to social affairs in Reno.

One day while dining at the Riverside Hotel with some eastern friends of her mother's, one of the women was making a great fuss over the little eight-year-old, saying what a darling little girl she was. "And I suppose," she said, "You have a dear little pony all your own?"

Much to her shocked surprise she heard from little puffy-ruffles, "Hell, no! The damned old bastard's fourteen years old."

The little girl had been after her father for some time to buy her a spirited horse like the one he rode, and the eastern lady had touched upon a tender subject and gotten a child's honest answer.

It had been years since we'd filed our claim on Tom's desert land, and we had made many improvements. Daddy had drawn a map of the claim, showing the location of the springs and alfalfa fields, and had sent it to Washington, D.C., with a request for the title. Several years passed, and we wondered what was holding up the title, and we were getting a little worried about the delay. One day a man drove out in a big car and came to the door acting very officious and stern, and inquired for Mr. Olds.

Daddy had gone to town that morning with the team and wagon. I told the gentleman that Daddy wouldn't be back for three days, but perhaps I could answer his questions. He told me that he was a government agent from the Land Office in Washington, D.C., and had been sent out to inspect the improvements on our desert claim. He would decide whether our request for a title would be granted or refused. I gladly and rather proudly showed him the land. I took him to our tunnel and had him walk back into it, and I showed him irrigated fields and the fencing.

When he finished the inspection he had a big smile on his face. "Well, this is one on Uncle Sam," he said. "The men in the U.S. Land Office think of desert land as being flat, level country, and they couldn't understand your husband's map and his explanation of running a tunnel into a hill to irrigate a field below. It just couldn't be done." After waiting and debating it for three years they had sent this man clear across the country to evict Mr. Olds from that land. Then he added, "I just wish I could show the fellows in Washington your tunnel and that alfalfa field. I guarantee you'll receive your title as soon as I get back to Washington."

The title arrived in the mail shortly after. We now had two hundred and eighty acres of land and a four-room house. We were still gaining and prospering slowly but surely.

]{ **Sixteen**]{

In 1916 the rabies broke out among the coyotes in the West. From the first rumor, the government realized the seriousness of the situation and must have spent thousands of dollars on literature. We were about as small a ranching outfit as anyone could be, but each mail day brought a government bulletin telling all about the progress of the rabies, its symptoms, and its reaction on cattle and other animals infected.

I was particularly interested in its reaction on cattle, as we now had about fifty head. There was one purebred red Durham bull, of which I was especially proud. We had bought him as a yearling and had paid all our year's savings for him. To me, the bull represented the coming realization of my dreams. Someday we were going to get out of the home-steader class. The name homesteader, or "nester" as we were called, was an insult to me—a moniker of inferiority. I had overheard our children being called "nester's brats," but with our herd growing and our purebred bull, we would soon be known as cattlemen, owners of the Olds Cattle Ranch. I didn't want anything to happen to that bull. Daddy was bedfast most of the time that winter and wasn't much interested in the government reports. I was. I would bring each pamphlet into his bedroom and read it aloud.

He would say, "Oh, hell, old lady. Don't pay any attention to them. It's just some government scheme to get more money by raising taxes to start some new biological survey, or something of that kind."

I was worried from the very beginning, for I was proud of our little herd of cattle and didn't want the rabies to get among them. I read all the bulletins carefully so that I would be able to recognize the disease in case we had an outbreak.

Then one morning, Bob, the old blacksmith who worked for the PF outfit for twenty years and had started up his forge at five A.M. every morning of that twenty years, went out to start his forge and had had to kill a mad coyote with a pitch fork. Then with his lantern in his hand, he walked the two and a half miles to our house and warned me to keep the children in the yard and the dogs tied up. I was very worried and followed his advice.

Daddy thought it was all foolishness. "I'll bet, old lady," he said, "that that coyote Bob killed didn't have rabies. He probably went inside the shop for shelter from the cold." I didn't listen to Daddy, but for three weeks I kept the children in the yard and the dogs tied up. Soon after though, I became careless and turned both dogs and children loose.

Edson was working in Reno that winter, but he came home on weekends. One Sunday morning the little children were all outside the yard playing when all of a sudden they all came screaming into the house. "Mad coyote! Mad coyote!"

Through the open door we could see the animal. He had come within a few feet of where the children were playing, and was still standing there unperturbed by all the running and screaming. Hell broke loose in our kitchen, and I believe that's putting it mildly. We all lost our heads. I stood there clutching first one child and then another, and trying to put my arms around them all at once. "Where's Jessie? Where's Alice? Is Albert here? Get all five of them. Where're Leslie and Martha?" I kept thinking one of them was missing and must be out there with that mad coyote. The children couldn't be quieted but kept screaming, "Mad coyote!"

Edson was doing no better than I. He couldn't find the gun. The guns and ammunition were a part of our equipment that was always kept in one place—guns on a rack high on the bedroom wall where the children couldn't reach them, and the ammunition box directly under them. The rifle shells, being heavy, had sunk to the bottom of the box, and Edson in his frenzy couldn't find them. He grabbed the shotgun shells and the shotgun and out he went after the coyote, which still hadn't moved. Edson fired twice, both shots hitting the animal broadside, but the number eight shot wasn't strong enough to penetrate and kill it. It got away.

Edson trailed it by following the drops of blood in the snow. They led him down to the sheep ranch where Goshie was foreman. Edson told him about the mad coyote and told him to keep a lookout for it. Old Goshie had a queer habit of shrugging his shoulders, spreading out his hands and saying, "Maaybeee," when he couldn't quite believe what you were saying.

Now he shrugged and said, "Maaybeee, maybe coyote not mad—just sick?"

Edson came on home where the excitement, by now, had quieted down some. In about an hour, though, here came old Goshie, riding as fast as the horse could run. He talked fast and loud in Basque, French, and Spanish, but never a word in English. He was gesturing and ejaculating and babbling, and the only word we could understand was "borregos." We knew that was "sheep" in Spanish, and concluded from his excitement that the mad animal had gotten among his sheep.

Edson saddled up, took the rifle, which he was able to find shells for this time, and went home with Goshie. They found some of the sheep badly torn, but they never found the coyote.

Again we tied up the dogs and kept the children close in the yard for a few weeks. As time is a wonderful healer, so is it a good "forgetter," and again we relaxed our fears and precautions over the rabies. Then one morning while I was down at the stack yard feeding, I noticed one of our milk cows, Babe, standing off by herself. She wouldn't come to feed. I thought nothing of it at the time, but the next morning she was still standing in the same spot, in the same position. This attracted my attention.

She stood there with her head bowed toward her feet, and her tail was sticking straight up in the air, just as the bulletin had described the first stages of this disease. The first few days, I had read, a cow would go blind and stand in the position which Babe demonstrated. Then the tail would start winding and unwinding in a rhythmic motion. The tail motion would continue for a few days, and then the whole body would go into writhing convulsions. I exclaimed aloud, "Oh, dear God! Old Babe has the rabies!" She had every symptom described in the government bulletin. I hurried through my feeding, and ran to Daddy's bedside where I exclaimed, "Daddy, old Babe has rabies!" I got the bulletin and sat down beside his bed and read and explained to him, "That's exactly how Babe is acting."

Daddy said, "Aw, bosh, old lady. It's just your

imagination. Go down and drive her up and out here in the corral at the barn where you can feed her alone and watch her."

It's been said, "God takes care of fools and children." I was no child, but whether a fool or not, God took care of me. I got a long willow stick to guide her, as she was blind, and guided her by placing the stick first on one side of her head and then on the other, and I twisted her tail to make her go, talking to her all the time. I believe she understood what I said. She made no resistance whatever, but plodded slowly and painfully up to the corral. Here I fed her, and cut the ice in the watering trough so she could drink. I shut the gate and left her. Watching her carefully the next few days, I never saw her drink or eat. Every morning I opened the gate and went in to cut the ice.

On the third day when I went in, she broke out past me bawling and jumping and ran up the gulch a few hundred yards where she lay down. It was Sunday again and Edson had made plans to ride out with a friend to go hunting. I told him about Babe, read the pamphlet for the thousandth time, and explained it to him. I asked him to go and shoot her.

Daddy called out from his bed, "Don't shoot her, Edson. I think it's just the old lady's imagination."

Edson looked dubiously at me and said, "Well, it's Dad's cow."

"I don't care whose cow it is," I retorted. "You're not going back to town and leave me here with a sick man and a mad cow. Go on now and have your hunt, but save some shells so you can kill her when you get back."

About a half hour after the boys left, old Babe came down to the house, whether it was because she was a pet and wanted us to help her, or for what reason I don't know. She put on an awful death battle right in front of Daddy's window and not fifty feet away. She bellowed—not a regular cow's bawling, but the most maniacal bellow I've ever heard. She dug holes two feet deep in the ground with her hooves and horns. She chased birds, chickens, anything that moved, and her whole body twitched and writhed all the time. She kept this up for five hours!

We had the dogs and cats in the house, but all the children were over playing on the haystack. I yelled at them to stay there, but after an hour or two they got cold and wanted to come home. "No, sir!" I yelled at them. "Burrow down under the hay to keep warm, but don't dare come home."

The hunters hadn't found any game, but they had shot away all their shells but one, in target practicing. Then Edson happened to think of Ma's mad cow. Well, maybe she was mad. They'd better save that one shell. When they arrived home, Edson didn't have to be told to kill Babe. They had heard her bawling a half a mile away. When they came near enough Edson jumped off his horse and raised the gun ready to fire.

I was standing on the front porch with my hands clenched till the fingernails cut into the palms of my hand, praying, "God take care of my boy! God help my boy!" She saw him and charged.

Edson stood there smiling, gun raised, with Babe bearing down on him. He waited until she was a thin twenty feet from him, and then he fired. She went down. Edson put the lasso rope around her neck, and the dallies around the saddle horn and hauled her away into the high sagebrush. We all piled brush on top of her and cremated her according to government orders.

It was the tensest moment in my life when I stood on

the front porch and watched a mad cow bear down on my seventeen-year-old son. If I had known he had only one shell, I think I would have collapsed.

Now we worried about how many more of our cattle had been bitten by the coyote. We worried even more about how we would kill them without any rifle shells. Edson said he'd send out a box of shells through the mail and we'd get them next mail day—the following Saturday. Since this was only Sunday we had a whole week of suspense in front of us. We could only hope there would be no more outbreak of rabies in our herd.

But the very next morning when I went down to feed, there stood our prize bull, head down at his feet, tail in the air, standing in the very spot Babe had stood. I cried aloud, "Oh, my God, no! Not our prize bull!" But there he stood. It could be nothing else but rabies. I went on feeding, and then I went up to Daddy and told him what I had found. I asked him if he didn't have strength enough to get up and go down and kill the bull.

He said, "No. There's nothing to kill him with except the shotgun and number eight shot. It can't be done."

I didn't force the issue, but I knew that someway we had to kill the bull, and the sooner the better. Next day when I went down to feed, the bull hadn't moved. Right then I went on strike. I went back to the house and into Daddy's bedroom. "Daddy, you'll have to get up and come kill that bull. I won't feed another spear of hay until you do. There's no need letting him go through the same torture old Babe did. He might kill some of the stock or even one of the children! I believe if you hold the shotgun right next to his body over the heart that the shot will penetrate it and kill him."

Daddy got up and dressed. He was very wobbly and insecure on his feet. As we went down to the meadow he had to lean heavily on my shoulder, and I carried the gun. When we walked up to the mad bull, I was right beside Daddy to protect him if anything unexpected happened. He placed the muzzle of the gun on the hide just behind the left shoulder and fired both barrels. The bull went down and got to his feet again while Daddy was reloading. He gave him two more barrels in the same place. The bull staggered and wobbled across the meadow and into the high sagebrush a quarter of a mile away. Then he fell. I left Daddy there while I followed across the meadow to see if the animal was dead. I kicked him and punched him with a stick, and he didn't move, so I went back to Daddy, pronouncing the bull dead, and helped Daddy back to the house.

It was a slow process, as it was steeply uphill all the way, and he had to sit down and rest several times. I thought surely every rest he took would be his last, and I blamed myself for everything. Why had I insisted on him getting up to shoot the bull? Why didn't I have guts enough to shoot it myself? I berated myself all the way back to the house. At last I got him back to bed, resting comfortably.

At four P.M. when school was out the teacher and I and the children went down to the meadow and began piling sagebrush on the bull. The bull was a shorthorn Durham, and he had fallen with one horn sticking in the soil, with his nose touching the ground. Before we began the brush piling, I built a little pile of grass and fine sticks under his head, with which to start my fire. When we had the sagebrush piled as high as we could throw it, I parted the brush carefully, and crawled on my hands and knees to the bull's head, where I lit a match and set the grass on fire.

Just then that bull raised his head and let out a maniacal bellow! I had gone in carefully, so as not to disturb our funeral pyre, but now I came out of there

screaming at the top of my lungs and throwing sagebrush in every direction. I grabbed the four-year-old
baby, Martha, by the hand, and we all ran as if the devil
was after us. We never looked around or stopped until
we got outside the meadow fence where we sat down
and held a counsel as to what we had done and what we
were going to do now. It was evident that the bull had
just strength enough left to raise his head and bellow.
There was nothing to fear from him now.

Eight-year-old Albert was the next man on the place.
I sent him up to Daddy. "Have him tell you exactly
where to hold the gun so we can kill that bull this time."

Daddy had already given Albert lessons in shooting,
but he had never let him take the gun out alone. "Tell
Daddy to give you the gun, and you come back here,
and we'll all go down to help you shoot the bull," I told
him.

When Albert came back with the gun, we all joined
hands, making quite a string of us, and went down to
where the bull lay. We unpiled the sagebrush, and
Albert held the gun just back of the left shoulder, firing
both barrels. We could see the bull's muscles relax and
straighten out. He was really dead this time. Then we
repiled the sagebrush and went ahead with the cremation. I was never so scared out of my wits as when the
supposedly dead bull raised his head and bellowed at
me.

Before the rabies died out we lost five head. We
became so methodical about killing them that we
destroyed them at the first sign of the disease. I have
often wondered since what would have happened if we
had been using the milk from Babe when she became
infected, but luckily she was dry at the time.

Seventeen

All the children seemed anxious to be allowed to go to Constantia for the mail, eighteen miles away. Each one in turn started carrying mail when only eight years old—that is, they rode thirty-six miles on an unchaperoned trip.

All the time they were growing up we thought they enjoyed those trips. Years later, however, on overhearing a conversation between two of my grown daughters, it dawned on me that their mail-carrying trips were shows of sheer courage rather than pleasure. They would see carcasses of dead animals with their eyeballs eaten out by buzzards, who would get to them almost as soon as the critter would die. The eyeballs were the only part of an animal the buzzards could get until a coyote had torn the hide and exposed the flesh.

Along the mail route there was a ten mile strip of road uninhabited by human beings, but there were many buzzards. Along this strip the buzzards would fly from one telephone pole to another, keeping just ahead of the children. In their flighty imagination the children thought the birds were keeping just ahead of them, watching for them to fall off and get killed so they could go on with their ghoulish feast of eyeballs. They always raced their horses across that lonely stretch of country.

One spring, after a heavy winter of snow, a sheepherder over at Fort Sage, twelve miles from our place, found a piece of quartz float that showed free gold. Knowing little about minerals, but thinking he had something good, he saddled up his pack mule and rode into Reno with the piece of rock. Having it assayed, he found it to be very rich in gold.

The news spread fast and grew to gigantic proportions. The evening paper told of the rich gold strike at Fort Sage, and the whole town was alive with enthusiasm. I happened to make a trip to Reno the same day the sheepherder arrived with the float, and I read in the paper all about the rich strike. I thought nothing of it at the time, but bought my usual supply of groceries, and on the second day I started home only to find the road swarming with people.

It looked as though the whole population was going prospecting and on their way to a rich strike. There were Reno businessmen, lawyers, doctors, miners, and old prospectors. They had hired every conceivable conveyance from four-in-hand coach down to the old prospector's pack burro.

Had I been a drinking woman I could have indulged in a big, free drunk, for all the passersby thought I, with my big bill of grub on the wagon, was going out to the strike to start a boarding house, and they all hailed me with, "Hey, lady! Stop and have a drink to the success of your boarding house."

I refused their drinks, but I did stop at Dry-Bone Lake to have a cup of coffee and a ham sandwich with an old prospector. The aroma of the ham frying and the coffee brewing out in the open air was too tempting to pass.

The rich strike never materialized. Nothing was

ever found after the rich piece of float picked up by the sheepherder. Thus ended another fabulous gold strike.

When I got back with my bill of grub, I had to ride out after two steers that I had designated as strays. I did all my own riding after cattle, and I had a little system all my own of keeping track of our herd. They were out on the open range on Tule Mountain, and twice a week I rode out to check them. All my she-stock was named, and I designated the steers as progeny of such and such a branch. I kept a regular roll of all the she-stock, which I took with me when I rode out to check them. Each cow that I didn't see would get a check after her name—the same with the steers. When there were three checks after one name, I would designate that one as a stray and would put in some time looking for it. I also told all the cowboys passing our way that one of our critters was lost and asked them to keep an eye out for it.

There were two steers that I hadn't seen for some time, and I was beginning to worry about them. Edson came in one evening and said that the cowboys from the Winnemucca Ranch had driven in a big herd and that our two steers were among them. "They're in the field down by the meadow, Ma. If you'll come with me, we can work them through the PF stack yard and get them home."

School was just out, and I was getting supper. I turned the cooking over to Jessie, and went to help get the steers. When we got there, we turned a number of PF cows into the stack yard along with our steers. We cut the steers out, and Edson followed to herd them, for it was difficult to get them away from the stack yard. I turned the PF bunch back, and got off my horse to close the gate when an old cow spied me. A range cow hates a human being on foot, and she took in after me.

Edson saw her the same time I did and hollered, "Run, Ma! For God's sake, run! She's after you!"

I wasn't waiting to be told to run. I was doing my best to save my hide. I made for a fence about sixty feet away. Edson was on the other side and had jumped off his horse and gotten down on his knees in order to pull me through the barbed wire in case my clothes caught.

I could feel that cow's breath down the back of my neck, and the thought flashed through my mind, "I can't go through that barbed wire. My riding skirt will catch and she'll hit me about middle rear." When I reached the fence I put my hand on top of the post and gave what seemed to me to be just a light spring. I went sailing over the top of five strands of barbed wire.

As I landed, I turned to see that the old cow had stopped. Edson was still on his knees, rocking back and forth with laughter and clapping his hands. "Good Lord, Ma, you could have jumped it if it had been six strands. You cleared it by two feet!"

I passed that hay corral many times since, and I used to stop and wonder how I ever cleared it. I know now how I did it. I did my very best, and God did the rest.

Shortly after the fence-jumping episode, I was riding on the mountain after cattle when I happened on a scene that could have been a tragedy.

Two cowboys, Bud and Maverick, were riding along the rim rocks of a deep canyon. They saw an eagle fly over the cliff and land in a scrub sagebrush about thirty feet down the sheer wall. The boys' curiosity was aroused. Neither of them had ever seen a young eagle. They talked it over, wondering how to get a close-up look at the nest, and soon devised a plan. Since Maverick was a small man, they would tie the lasso rope around his waist and Bud would take a half-hitch around a juniper tree with the free end of the rope and lower Maverick down over the cliff. When he reached the desired spot, Maverick was to holler.

I arrived at that moment, just in time to see the fun—for as it happened, it was fun. Bud had lowered Maverick down the cliff wall and was very carefully playing out the rope, when all at once we heard an awful howl, "Let go! Let go! You blankety-blank old son of a bitch! I tell you, let go!"

Bud, unable to see over the cliff, and hearing Maverick use those endearing terms, thought that he could be speaking to no one but him. He obeyed orders, and threw over the rope, letting Maverick drop a straight two hundred feet down the cliff! Fortunately the scrub sage that grew out of the sides of the cliff wall broke his downward speed, and he landed badly scratched, but safe.

Bud and I looked over the cliff and hollered, "Are you all right?" We heard his answer, "Yes." We hurried to lead the horse a mile down the country, and back up the canyon, where the badly scratched Maverick was waiting for us, and laughing.

He told us how it had happened. When he came opposite the eagle's nest he reached out his hand to shoo the bird off. Instead of shooing, she reached out and clamped two of his fingers in her beak. She bore down with such force that he couldn't pull them away. Of course, it had been the eagle he was yelling at in pain. "Well, anyway," he said, "I got my fingers out of the eagle's beak." It all ended in a good, hearty laugh.

I know from experience how fierce an eagle can be, for I still carry the scar on my leg from the talons of the eagle that I trapped.

Maverick had come by his odd name naturally. He had come as a hired hand from the orphanage, not belonging to anyone; the cowboys had called him Maverick as a nickname, and it stuck. It was a natural name, for maverick is the name they give to un-branded calves in the south, just as we call them leppes in this part of the country. He's now a man of sixty-five and I don't believe I've ever heard any name for him but Maverick.

Cowboy Fred, who later became my son-in-law, was riding with me one day at noontime, for at that time of the day the cows all came in to the watering place to rest and get out of the heat. It was a good time to check them, so we waited by the watering hole.

Fred said, "Mom, do you understand cow lan-guage? Listen. You see that big bull, the Monarch of the Range, coming down the trail with his head held low? He's saying in a mumbling way, 'I'mmm gooooin' to tooown! I'm gooooin' to tooown!' "

Then he pointed to a young bull coming down the side trail bawling away with his head pointed up. "See him? He says, 'Me tooooo!' Then over on the other side—that young bull running—he's saying, 'Leeet's all goooo! Leeet's aaall goooo!' Mom, that's cow language, and you can imagine that that's what they're really saying."

Eighteen

Our school journal, the *Tule Mountain Record*, which the children began to print when we got our school, carried every bit of the news in the neighborhood. In looking back through the old copies, which I've always kept, I found some interesting and amusing items which have been almost forgotten. This story appears in one of the papers:

"The cowboys had great fun in playing practical jokes on one another, but they especially loved to have a joke on a new cowhand. In this instance, they had driven a bunch of steers to town, and as it was a long drive, they took along the chuck wagon, and the camp cook, whose name was Jones. It naturally followed, that his nickname was Casey Jones.

"While in town, they hired a new hand, a big Dutchman named Spider, who rode home in the wagon with Casey. They told Spider (he never went by any other name), that Casey was subject to fits after he'd been in town drinking, and they gave him a bottle of 'medicine' composed of tea and vinegar, telling him to force the liquid down Casey's throat if he should throw a fit. Next they drew Casey aside, and told him to throw a fit, so they could have a little fun scaring Spider.

"About ten miles out on the desert, Casey threw the fit, and Spider, according to orders, advanced on

Casey with the bottle. A hard struggle ensued. The Dutchman was the stronger man, and he downed Casey, hog-tied him, and forced every drop of the 'medicine' down his throat. The rest of the boys managed to overtake them, and Casey didn't have to ride hog-tied very long.

"Next day, they turned the tables and played a joke on Spider. While branding some new bulls, they turned the last one loose while Spider stood nearby. When the bull charged him, he stood his ground, waving his hands, and shouting at the animal, 'Vait! Vait a minute! Vait now!'

"The boys were all yelling at him to run, and finally he took their advice. Just as he reached the fence, the bull knocked him down. One of the boys reached under the fence and pulled him to safety. He got up, a very angry Spider, and wanted to fight the whole bunch of cowboys.

"They laughingly told him it was just a joke. 'Yoke?' yelled the Dutchman, 'You call that a yoke?' "

Another article in the *Record*:

"The cowboy boss, who came with four mules and the chuck wagon, picked up the teacher, and Alice, and Jessie, who are now thirteen and fifteen years of age, and took them to a dance across Tule Mountain at the Fish Springs Ranch. There was a high summit to cross, and it was snowing when they left home, but thinking it to be just a small flurry, they started in plenty of time to make the twenty-five-mile distance before nightfall. They had no trouble in getting there, but the storm continued, and they stayed at the ranch until the storm was over. The snow was so deep on the summit, that they had to drive eighty miles around the foot of the mountain to get home. They lost three days of school, which had to be made up at the end of the term."

In the spring, I supplemented our meat supply by raising "bummer" lambs. When an old ewe has twin lambs, and has milk enough for only one, she butts the other one away from her, and won't let it come near her again. The sheepherder either has to kill the lamb or give it away. One can acquire any number of bummers during lambing time. It took me a long time to learn the formula to feed them, and many's the pet lamb that I have cried over losing.

The following is an illustrated item, which appeared in the *Record*, written by Leslie, who was then only ten:

"Item: The sheep ranch at Tule is slowly by surely increasing and decreasing. The death list for the night of April 11, was one dearly beloved Fluff, dead of pneumonia, and for April 13, Goshie and Milkman — the latter mourned by Jessie Olds, will long be remembered among the angels."

In starting a new school year, this poem appeared in the *Record* written by Leslie:

> On this September twenty-first
> We start a brand new year,
> And welcome *Tule Record*
> With loud hurrahs and cheer.
>
> With grins that stretch from ear to ear,
> Eyes bright with happy tears,
> We'll start the *Record* once again —
> Dear diary of the years.

Some of the cowboys were pretty fair poets, and they often brought their own contributions to our paper. We had a reading of the paper one evening every two weeks, and all the cowboys would attend, sometimes riding thirty or forty miles to listen to each other's literary efforts. The teacher at the Dry Valley School brought her children for the social evening, for they often had contributions in our journal, as well.

The cowboy boss had quite a case on our school-mom, and one of the boys who was poetically inclined sent in this poem:

Ode To A Cowboy

Here's to the PF buckaroo boss, rider of fame,
I guess you all know him. Bucko's his name.
He can throw a big loop way up in the air,
And at bustin' wild broncs, he is always there.

He's now going to school at the Olds' farm,
Of course, an education will do him no harm.
But he started to win the schoolmom's heart
With a span of wild mules and a breaking cart.

How he's making out we don't quite know,
But we're inclined to think he's a little bit slow,
For the other day we heard by chance,
That the schoolmom's lover is over in France.

But nevertheless if he's made a mistake,
He can always go back to Honey Lake,
To his desert girl, who is waiting there,
With her freckled face and her bright red hair.

The poem brought quite a laugh, for all the boys had managed to be there. Needless to say, it didn't bring a smile from the teacher—it was too true.

Another article contributed by the cowboys was illustrated by Alice and went like this:

EXTRA!

"Mr. Rudolph Buckou, while riding near Nixon, reached the banks of the Truckee River just in time to

save the life of a drowning cowboy. Only for Mr.
Buckou's presence of mind and very skillful roping
both horse and rider would have drowned.

"Joe Overalls, chief of the Indian Tribe, has
awarded Mr. Buckou a medal for his heroic bravery.

From A. Reader"

Our evenings spent reading the *Tule Mountain Record* reminded me of the country literary societies that
we had back in Iowa when I was a girl. As long as we
had children in school the *Tule Mountain Record* continued to be published, and I cherish it to this day.

As recorded in our journal, I raised "bummer"
lambs for our summer's meat. The big sheep ranch
below us afforded us as many lambs as we could
raise, which was usually ten or twelve. If I raised
more than we needed, I could always sell the surplus.

We had to do a lot of scheming in order to have
lamb to eat, for the children made pets of every one,
naming them, each one choosing one special lamb for
his own particular pet. They were very dear little
animals, and the children would not allow any of
them to be killed. Finally we derived a plan, with old
Goshie's help, so that we could have lamb to eat
without killing the children's pets. We would trade
our lamb with a field lamb that Goshie had raised. We
left all our lambs at his ranch, and he would kill and
dress some of his lambs and trade them for ours.

It was a wonderful scheme, for the children could
always go down to Goshie's and play with their pets.
After the lambs were grown and turned out on the
range with a band of sheep, the children would go
into the band of sheep and call the name of their own
pet. They couldn't recognize their own animal after it
was full-grown, but the lambs never forgot the chil-

dren. They would call, "Here Fluff! Here Speckles!" and out would come a full-grown sheep to be loved and petted.

We used to take a walk every evening out to what we called the "turkey tree," just a mile from the house. The "turkey tree" is the one on which Edson hung the turkey for coyote bait on our first Thanksgiving on the homestead. We had built a road out across the flat past the "turkey tree," which cut off a distance of two miles on our way to Reno. The tree was the end, or turning spot, in our walks. Just past that tree we would all count in unison, "One, two, three, turn!" and back we'd go.

Our walk across the flat made a queer looking procession. There was the teacher, myself, the children, the dogs (never less than three), a kitten for each of the children to carry, and the lambs, following us like dogs.

One evening on our walk, Connie, an old shepherd dog, scared a killdeer off her nest. I followed the bird, fascinated by the way she flopped along on the ground pretending to have a broken wing, to lure us away from her nest.

Suddenly, I heard one of the children call, "Connie, drop that!" I looked around just in time to see one of the strangest sights I have ever seen. Connie had picked up two baby killdeer, and had been holding them in her mouth.

When she heard the command, she opened her mouth, and out walked what looked like two balls of fluff on toothpicks. The baby birds walked right down the dog's long, red tongue and jumped to the ground uninjured.

I saw another illustration of "the survival of the

fittest." One morning the children and I were going over to the far garden where there was a spring and a little reservoir that irrigated about an acre of ground. We raised an abundance of vegetables and two rows of currant and gooseberry bushes. (I think I've made enough jelly from the fruit of those bushes so that if it was all melted up in one gob it would float a battleship.)

A little brown thrush had built a nest in one of the currant bushes by the garden gate. The children were interested in the nest from its first beginning of a few pieces of straw and horsehair. We could never pass the nest without each one of them parting the bushes and taking "just one tiny peek," while the parent birds would fly scolding around their heads, pecking and chattering. They admired the five little brown-speckled eggs when they were laid, and when the babies were hatched out, they were wild with joy and thought they were beautiful—a child's stretch of imagination, for to my notion, there is nothing uglier than a newly hatched bird. There are no feathers, and there seems to be nothing to them except a big mouth and eyes. The children loved them anyway.

One morning, as we were on our way to the garden, but still some distance away, we heard the old birds making an awful chatter, and knew there was something after the babies.

Albert said, "Mama, if that's a gopher snake after our birds, may we kill it?" He asked permission, for we had earlier resolved not to kill gopher snakes.

I gave them permission, and away they went much faster than I. Sure enough it was a gopher snake. It had gathered several currant stalks together and wrapped its body round and round them like the stripes on a barber pole. He crawled up the stalks till there were about twelve inches of his body free so that he could sway over the nest and gulp down the birds. Albert chopped the snake's head off with the garden hoe, and there was mute evidence of his deed. There were two big bumps about half way down the length of his body where he was digesting two little birds. There was another bird in his mouth that dropped out uninjured when Albert cut off the snake's head.

The children picked up the baby and after each one had fondled it, they put it back into the nest. All three of the remaining baby birds grew to maturity and flew away.

This was a queer little insight into nature, that only we of the great open spaces have access to and have the pleasure of seeing.

About 1920 we had a very early spring and the grass was in abundance all over the hills; but as early grass is weakening to cattle we were still feeding them on hay, opening the gate only occasionally to let them graze on the new grass. One day two of our heavy heifers strayed away and enjoyed the grass so much that they didn't come back to feed on hay. I began riding out to look for them. They had already calved when I found them and were thin and weak and needed feed. As a range cow always hides her calf for a few days, I made several unsuccessful rides trying to find the cows and calves together.

Being determined to get them in to feed, I started out one morning just before daylight to where they were ranging seven miles from home. As I rode along in the early dawn the lovely pink rays of sunrise tipped the crest of Dogskin Mountain. Soon I reached a little meadow where there were a few acres of grass topped on the upper side by a snow bank that was melting and running down in little rivulets on the meadow. When I first arrived everything was quiet and still.

I stopped my horse and sat in the stillness, rejoicing in the beauty of nature. An old hymn came to my mind called "In The Silence":

> In the beauty and stillness, I find sweet repose
> When God and my soul are alone.

I sat fascinated, watching the sun come up while all nature awakened. I saw a wild crocus come into full bloom. It had come through the ground with its stem doubled up, just as a bean pushes through the earth. Slowly, as I watched, the stem began to straighten and one end broke loose from the ground. The tiny flower raised its head while one petal after another unfolded, and when the stem was fully straightened the flower was in full bloom. All around me things were awakening and coming to life.

Crickets came out of the cracks in the earth and made their merry little "chirit cheree." Down to my left in the lower corner of the meadow a flock of valley quail came in out of the sagebrush, and were busily scratching and calling "cucoocoo, cucoocoo," to one another. Farther over, where the meadow met the adjoining hill, were a flock of mountain quail giving their shrill whistle to each other.

Perched on a granite boulder out where the sagebrush met the sky was a cock sage hen strutting back and forth making that thunderous sound with his wings for the benefit of his little brown mate, who was daintily walking back and forth with her head cocked admiringly to one side as she glanced up at her lord.

Out in the sagebrush to the right of me two coyotes crept stealthily along with the big male in the lead. He stopped, squatting on his haunches, and threw his head back to let out an exuberant howl. All nature was waking up to spring.

I had spent an interesting and inspiring hour, and it was with reluctance that I left that beautiful mountain scene and rode on over the hill into the sunrise to find my young heifers giving their calves breakfast. I had arrived early enough this time, and I drove them home to their own meadow where I fed them and closed the gate so that they wouldn't get away again. I got up to the house in time to get breakfast and get the children into school at nine o'clock after making a fourteen mile ride.

The accomplishment was nothing, but my early morning ride is one of my dearest homesteading memories.

Nineteen

We had purposely left high sagebrush for protection from the wind on the outside of the west fence of the home garden and yard. One day as Daddy passed the garden on his way up from irrigating, he saw something interesting.

Hurrying to the house he called to me, "Come quick, old lady, if you want to see something good!" He took me by the hand and hurried me down to the garden fence. Peering through the sagebrush, we saw Albert, six, and Martha, four, standing beside the newly dug grave of a half-buried doll. They were holding up between them a small Montgomery Ward sales catalogue, which they had salvaged from our out-house. They were using it for a song book and conducting a funeral.

They were singing "Hi Diddle Diddle" and "Sweet Betsy From Pike" for funeral songs, their little faces struck with grief. Daddy and I watched awhile and then quietly slipped away. Later the children dug up the broken doll and brought it to me to mend.

The children had a special burying ground on a grassy plot near a spring some distance from the house. Here they conducted funerals for all their badly broken dolls and pets and buried them. Mostly there were dogs, cats, and lambs, and sometimes a little bird, which had fallen out of a tree and been killed. Each grave was marked with an Indian relic they had scouted the country to find. They held these "tombstones" as something sacred and would no more remove one from a grave than they would have removed a marker from a human grave.

Years later when they were all grown and gone and we had sold the ranch, we made a visit to the old homestead, and much to their sorrow and consternation we found that the tombstones had all been removed.

Most of the riding after cattle was done during the summer when the boys were away working, and since the girls were out of school, they helped me. The PF cowboys continued to help us with the branding, and the girls and I went along to help all we could. My job was doing the cooking, for though I was quite a hand with the pots and pans, I wasn't much help with a rope and branding iron.

There was a big picket corral at the top of Tule Mountain where we branded the spring and summer calves. One summer we went up to brand and found the corrals burned down. This meant we had to brand in the open, which necessitated the help of all hands, even the cook, in holding and branding.

Usually they sent one of the boys with me back to the camp to help me with the dutch oven, but this time they couldn't spare anyone, and I had to go back alone to get dinner for the bunch. The boys had moved camp that morning, putting all provisions on the ground, and erecting a tent over them.

I had brought along fresh raspberries to make them a pie and was down on my knees in the tent, with my back to the tent opening, patting a pie dough into a pan. I was wearing Levi's that day, instead of the usual riding skirt. Suddenly, I was rudely surprised. The tent flap was flung open, and someone applied a boot to the seat of my pants and said, "Hey, there, you damned old son of a bitch! Is dinner ready?"

Looking around I said, "Well, just about." There stood a young cowboy kid about eighteen years old. He was completely surprised and embarrassed to see me. He grabbed off his big cowboy hat and stammered out, "Forgive me, lady! For God's sake forgive me! I didn't know there was a woman within twenty miles of here. Please forgive me!"

"Just forget it, kid. Can you run a dutch oven? If so, I think God might have sent you. Get out there and dig a trench big enough for four ovens and it will help me a lot." He dug the trench, gathered wood, and built a fire in it, and when the wood burned down to a bed of coals, he shoveled them all out. I was ready with my four ovens. One oven was filled with sage hen, one with biscuits, one with vegetables, and the last with my special berry pie. We set the ovens in the hot trench and covered them with coals. Then we sat on the hill side and talked while they baked.

We talked about everything. Every few minutes, he would break out with, "Please don't tell the other boys about me. They'd never quit raggin' me about it!" I promised again and again not to tell, but he kept making the same request and remained uneasy and fidgety. At last the bunch came in view over the rim rocks and headed down toward camp for dinner. There were seven cowboys and my three girls. I had to go into the tent for some last minute preparation, and when I returned the young cowboy was just stepping into his saddle. He tipped his big hat and waved good-bye to me. He rode down the canyon, and I never saw him again. He didn't have faith enough in women to trust me not to "squeal" on him.

I kept his secret for several years, when one day I was talking to my son-in-law, who had been cowboy boss at that time. I told him of my funny experience, and he told me that the kid was the son of an old friend of his and was to have met him at the cow camp on that appointed day. Evidently he had mistaken me in my Levi's for the boss. He had often wondered why the boy hadn't showed up.

The dance at Fish Springs was the first dance away from home ever attended by our girls, and it was the forerunner of many that followed. Women were scarce in our part of the country. A Spanish family named Giraldo were our neighbors, living twelve miles away over in Dry Valley. There were four boys and an adorable girl named Adelaide, who was the age of my daughter, Jessie. She was a typical Spanish type with dark skin, large brown eyes, two long heavy braids of black hair, and she was the jolliest, happiest person I have ever met. Her happiness grew up with her, and her philosophy of life has always been, "If you can't fix a thing, skip it." How much happier we would all be, if we could make that philosophy work in our own lives. Adelaide and my two older girls were great companions and many a horseback ride they had across that twelve-mile stretch, and many are the dances we've had with myself, my bunch, Adelaide, and the Dry Valley schoolteacher constituting the female attendance. We had to travel a good many miles to attend some of the neighboring dances. There was the Duck Lake school twenty-five miles away, over the line in California;

Bird Flat school, also in California, forty-five miles away; Doyle, twenty-eight miles; and our best dances at Flanigan, twenty-five miles away at the junction of the Western and the Pacific railroads. There the whole population of the different school districts would meet for an evening's fun. One old neighbor played the violin (he had a handle-bar mustache, and Alice was always waiting for it to get tangled in his fiddle strings), some of the cowboys brought their guitars, and Edson played the accordion. We all brought a cake and coffee and had a midnight supper, but there was never any charge, and we always danced till daylight. At daylight our group would go home with the cowboys to the camp for breakfast, and we always stayed to watch the boys mount their horses and start out on their day's ride. Many a good bucking horse show we've witnessed in those early morning hours.

It was nearly always a two days' trip to attend one of those dances, even after we got our Model-T Ford, for the trips to Flanigan, Duck Lake, or Fish Springs necessitated a trip over Fish Springs Hill, a very steep grade, which the Ford would not pull. We would drive as far as the car would go, and the boys would meet us there. We drained the radiator in a milk can brought along for the purpose. Then the cowboys would drive us with the buckboard and mules to wherever the dance was to be held, and then drive us back to the car the next morning after breakfast. Then they'd help us build a sagebrush fire to melt the ice in the milk can, get the car started, and see us on our way. It was some work to attend those dances, but we always came home feeling we'd had a wonderful time.

Besides being fun it was a handy and interesting way of keeping track of our stray cattle. People attended the parties from all parts of the range, and we always kept track of each other's strays.

It was always great fun for our teachers to go to the country dances, where everyone danced for the sheer joy of it. In some way, we always kept up to the latest popular dances. When I was a girl, we only danced the waltz, the schottish, the square dance, and of course, the sedate old varsuvia. Now they were dancing the fox trot, the turkey trot, and the one-step, or rag. I thought the new wiggly dances were terrible, but I tried the one-step and found it lots of fun.

We had great plans for one dance that never materialized. We had a schoolmom who had just come out from Reno to teach our school. The cowboy boss, Bowlegged Ed, came over and announced that he wanted to give a dance down at Goshie's where there was a big dining room. He said he would invite everyone on his coming ride to the different parts of the range. We set the date, and Ed made the verbal invitations. The teacher sent home for a party dress, which turned out to be a beautiful, blue evening gown. Our children were simply goggle-eyed over it, for it was the first formal dress they had ever seen. They told Ed about the beautiful dress, and showed it to him on his next visit to our place. Ed didn't say a word, but in the next day or two he rode around on that seventy-mile trip and uninvited all the people he had formerly invited.

When I asked him what made him do such a thing, he said, "I knew there wasn't any of the cowboys would want to dance with a schoolmom in a silk evenin' gown. Not when we all come in Levis." Not having the dance was a great disappointment to our little teacher, but she soon learned, "When in Rome, do as the Romans."

In the fall of 1918, the World War was in swing, and it was nearly impossible to get help. Fortunately for us, we had reared our own help, but a young couple who homesteaded near us, Mr. and Mrs. Griffin and their two-year-old baby, could get no one to help them. They were living in a tent on their property, and had cleared and fenced five acres of good land and planted it in potatoes. Then Mr. Griffin went away to work, leaving his wife Minnie to tend the potatoes. This she did faithfully with a garden hoe for her only implement. Water was scarce and had to be turned often on new rows of potatoes. I saw her every night all summer coming down the hill with her lantern at eleven P.M. and three A.M. to turn the water.

In the fall when the potatoes had to be harvested, it presented quite a problem. Mr. Griffin didn't like to quit his job to come home and harvest the crop. He had each weekend off, but instead of digging potatoes on those weekends he would go into town and try to hire help. He spent several weekends that way, but it was impossible to get help. It soon got to be November, and winter was almost upon us. I began to worry about that potato crop. I thought of all the hard work Minnie had done in raising it. It would be a shame to see her lose them.

Then a generous thought struck me. Here we were snug for the winter with all our crops harvested. Daddy was feeling pretty well, and Edson was home every Saturday and Sunday. Why not volunteer our help? With our team, plow and horses, we could all help dig their crop—even the schoolteacher.

I would like to be able to write an ode to country

teachers. I have never had one with me that wasn't willing to join wholeheartedly in my strange projects, anything from cremating a bull to helping the neighbors with their potatoes.

One Saturday when Mr. Griffin came home, the nine of us, Daddy and I, the teacher, and the six children, took up the plow and horse and went to work. We made short work of digging those potatoes. To make it a little more interesting, I offered a prize of five dollars to the one finding the largest potato. I found it myself the last day we worked. It was the largest I ever saw, weighing two pounds. Picking it up, I squealed with delight and called, "Isn't this fun?"

Jessie who was picking along with me said, "Mama, you can think the queerest things are fun! My back aches, my eyes are full of dirt, and my fingers are sore. I intend to stay with this job till it's finished, but it isn't a bit of fun!"

We finished digging the potatoes in two days, and buried them in a pit that had been dug previously. What a lucky thing for the Griffins that we did. That night a storm blew up and our real winter set in. Next spring potatoes sold for twelve dollars per hundred pounds, and the Griffins were able to make quite a profit on their crop.

⅜[**Twenty**]⅝

One spring when Alice and Jessie were in high school I found myself a little short on cash. I hadn't sold sage hens for a year or two, for there had been a law passed prohibiting the sale of them. Now I needed the money for the girls, so I had Daddy get me a couple of dozen birds. I knew it was unlawful, but needing the money I took the chance.

I had my birds all sold and most of them delivered when I was standing on a street corner talking to an old friend. A man I had sold some birds to walked by and nudged me with his elbow. Thinking it was an accident, I paid no attention to him. He turned and walking back he nudged me again. When I looked at him he grinned and winked. I thought, "Well, you old cuss! After knowing me all these years are you trying to get fresh with me?" I turned my back on him, but heard his footsteps clicking down the sidewalk, and I knew he turned and was headed back toward me. This time he gave me quite a jolt with his elbow and motioned for me to follow him.

As he stepped around the corner, I followed. I thought, "Old fella, I'll see what this is all about." He fell in step with me but never looked my way. Out of the corner of his mouth he said, "If you've got any sage hens in your car, for God's sake, dump 'em quick! The game warden's after you." He turned abruptly and left me.

I went down the street praying as I had never prayed before, "Oh, God, please don't let them send me to jail. I'll never sell another bit of game as long as I live!" I knew my high school girls would be terribly embarrassed if their mother was arrested. I did some fast walking, some quick thinking, and some fervent praying in the next few minutes. I dumped the birds and returned the money to those who had paid for them. That was years ago, and I've kept my promise never to sell game again, and I've been a law abiding citizen ever since.

After having bought the Merry Widow's ranch and the cabin from the Bartenders' Dream, we had enough lumber from the two houses on the property to add on to our own home. We made a long living room and two extra bedrooms, making seven rooms in all. Our schoolteacher had a room of her own, and the schoolroom was used solely for school.

Many's the dance and social affair we've held in our big living room. All the young folks from twenty and thirty miles around joined us in our fun. When our older girls, Jessie and Alice, were in high school in Reno then the place did become a popular place for dances. The girls would write out and say, "We're coming for a dance on Saturday night." Not "May we come?" but "We are coming." They would write to their many friends in the surrounding country and arrange to have them come. At the appointed time four or five cars of young folks from Reno could be spotted making their way toward the ranch. They always got there in time for supper, and the others would come later.

There was always plenty of music, for Edson played his accordion and one or two cowboys played the guitar. Sometimes we would wind up the phonograph and have a little canned music with someone standing by to keep it wound up. We would dance till midnight when I would serve coffee and cake. Then the dance continued until daylight, when most of the dancers would go home. Then the Reno boys and girls would take a nap . . . the boys retiring to the hay stacks, and the girls in any comfortable spot they could find around the house. They would awaken about three in the afternoon, have a big Sunday dinner and then go home. Although these parties were always lots of work for me, I enjoyed them as much as the girls did.

Sometimes the girls would bring a few friends out for Sunday dinner. One such time, I had a bunch of horses in the corral all ready to take on the mountain the next day. I was going to drive them over the top of the mountain and down into Mud Springs, three miles on the other side. By taking them over there, they wouldn't return home until roundup time in the fall.

I had just gotten the horses corralled at four P.M. on Saturday afternoon, when Leslie came in with the mail. In it was a letter from the girls saying they'd be home next day, Sunday, with some friends. "Please have dinner right at noon. We have to be back in town early," the letter read. They wanted me to have fried chicken and strawberry shortcake for dinner. It made things a little complicated for me, but I knew it could be done if I stretched the day a little.

At two A.M. Leslie and I started out with the horses. It was June, but going over the summit of

Tule we crossed a big snowbank. I thought, "If I could bring down some of that snow, I could make some homemade ice cream for the girls to go with their shortcake."

I nearly always carried a gunny sack over my saddle, but this time there was no sack on either saddle. My, how I wanted that snow! The ice cream would be such a treat for the girls and their friends. The rest of the way down to Mud Springs, I kept wondering to myself, "How can I get that snow?"

By the time I got back up to the snowbank, I had a way figured out. I always wear long underwear when riding on the mountain. This day, I was dressed in the usual riding skirt with each leg containing three yards of material. I took off the skirt and tore up a clean handkerchief for strings with which to hold the bottoms of the legs together. I then filled the legs of the skirt with snow, and tied it on the back of the saddle with the saddle strings. I rode the rest of the way home in my longies.

As we neared home, Leslie and I peeked around boulders and juniper trees to see if our company had arrived. If so, I would have to sneak in the back way. Fortunately there was no car in sight. We were cleaned up and dressed, with the dinner ready and the ice cream made when the happy, laughing company arrived. Leslie and I had made an eighteen mile ride and prepared dinner and dessert by the time the girls arrived, but as the storyteller would say, "A good time was had by all."

In 1917 we were about to lose our school. Jessie and Alice were in town at school, and Edson had quit several years before, thinking Ma needed his help more than he needed an education. That left only our three younger ones in school. If one of them should miss a day or two of school we would fall short of our daily attendance. Again came the big question, "What shall I do?"

I decided to stuff the school roll, that is, take in children to board, so that they could attend our school. I heard of a homesteader over in Red Rock Valley who had three little children but no school for them to attend. I drove over in the Ford and made arrangements to board his little girls from Monday to Friday without charge in order to have them on our school roll. It was cheaper for me to board his children on the ranch where we raised so much of our own food, than to have to give up the school and board our little ones in town.

In this way, I stuffed the school roll for five years until Leslie and Albert went to Reno for high school, leaving Martha in the sixth grade. Our state school superintendent received word that we had only one child of our own in school, and I was notified that the school would be closed. I made one more gallant try to hang onto the school.

I drove to Carson City to the superintendent's office and tried to talk him into continuing our school until the children could finish the grades. But my persuasiveness was to no avail. He pointed out that it was illegal and also very wrong if I had stuffed the roll with children whose parents did not live in our district. I didn't see it his way. The homesteader's children had no other chance at an education except what our little school offered them. I knew I had lost so I admitted, "I'm guilty, but I'm not a darn bit sorry. I only wish I could have held onto it in that way for two more years."

Our school was gone. We still had Leslie and Albert in high school and Martha not yet through the grades. I had promised myself to give the children a high school education at the very least. Daddy wanted to quit right there, but I refused. We were not going to quit until the last three children had a high school diploma. Some way we must keep on. I had a plan, but I wondered how I'd ever talk Daddy into agreeing to it. We always had such a difference in opinions.

I decided that I could rent a house in town for the winter and take in University girls to board. I figured that I could make enough to support the three children and myself with enough left over to hire a man to stay at the ranch with Daddy.

Things worked out my way. They were short on girls' dormitories and the dean of women was looking frantically for good homes in which to place girls. I rented a five bedroom house and obtained references as to my worth and ability from local businessmen, and the dean of women promised that she would fill my house for me.

I had gone ahead with my plans without a word to Daddy, but now I had to break it to him, for he had to sign the lease. My next problem was how to get him to do it. Again I had the feeling that I was doing right and that someway it would work out. I made an appointment with the landlord to meet him in town with my husband to sign the lease, and drove home.

I think Daddy and I came nearer to having a serious quarrel over that project than we ever had in our lives. I approached him saying, "Daddy I have a proposition to make—a plan I want to explain. Promise to keep still and listen without interrupting for three minutes. Then you have your say and I'll listen."

I talked fast, telling him everything I had done and ended by saying, "I want you to come in with me and sign that lease."

He listened, outwardly calm and unperturbed, and when I had finished he hit the roof! I confess I cheated. He had listened to me, but I turned a deaf ear on him for the next ten days. I never opposed him; I never answered him. The children and I began to put up the second crop of hay and get everything in order for the move to town. I felt confident that things would work out.

One day as I was topping out the last hay stack, our neighbors, the Jones family from twenty miles away, drove in to visit us. I called out to them, "Go on in and talk to Daddy for a few minutes. I'll be in to get dinner as soon as I finish this hay stack." When I finished the job I went into the house and sat in the living room to visit for a few minutes.

Almost the first thing Mrs. Jones said to me was, "I heard you lost your school, and I'm so sorry. What in the world are you going to do?" Right then I had an inspiration. "I'll let Daddy answer that question," I thought. I excused myself and hurried out to the kitchen to make a fire. I made lots of noise rattling the stove and banging pots and pans, but I kept one ear cocked to hear what was being said in the next room.

Just as I thought she would, Mrs. Jones repeated the question. To my delight I heard Daddy answer, "Well, by George, the old lady and I talked it over, and we decided that our last three children deserve an education the same as the rest. I have decided [I, mind you!] to send the old lady into Reno to run a student's boarding house. With what she earns there, and with the beef money from here, there'll be enough to support us and hire a man to take care of the ranch." There! I knew it would work out. The beauty of it was, Daddy thought it was all his decision.

He went in with me at the appointed time to sign the lease, and I was running a girls' boarding house. Financially, everything worked out well. I stayed the nine-month school term, but I was never so glad to get home in my life. I wasn't cut out to be a city dweller or a boarding-house keeper. I decided then that if ever I had to choose between hell and a girls' boarding house, that the boarding house would lose. I would never again leave Daddy and the ranch in someone else's care.

There would have to be some other way to get Albert and Martha through high school. But again a way was offered. The following year, Jessie was married and Martha went to live with her in Hawthorne, Nevada, finishing high school there. Albert worked his way through high school, paying his own way in town, and Leslie entered the University.

⸙| **Twenty-One** |⸙

After finishing high school and the two years normal school course at the University of Nevada, Jessie launched out on her teaching career. She was given a country school in White Pine County in country more desolate than where she was raised, and as it had been at our ranch it was a one family school for one homesteader in the district with a family of six children.

The schoolhouse was a half a mile from the homesteader's cabin, and there was a teacherage attached, forming an L-shaped building. Jessie wrote some very homesick letters, but she stayed with it. I realized it was a tough assignment for a young girl of twenty, and thought it would be easier for her if she could live with the family instead of half a mile from anybody. She got along fine until January when a real blizzard blew up. When the storm started, she dismissed school so that the children could get home, then busied herself getting in wood and preparing for the storm. When it started snowing she saw five horses move into the L where they were partly sheltered from the storm. After dark she could hear them milling and stamping in the snow.

It developed into a terrible blizzard, and she sat up feeding wood into the stove and listening to the wind until two A.M. when the door blew off the hinges. As she was trying to fasten the door shut by nailing a two-by-four across it, she heard someone calling, "Hallooo, halloo!"

It was the homesteader. He and his wife had become afraid that she would be frightened there alone and try to find her way to their place in the storm and get lost. He had brought along a big hand sled with which to carry the books and supplies back to the cabin so that they could hold school there until the storm was over and they could have access to the schoolhouse again. After nailing the door shut they sat by the fire and drank coffee by the gallon and listened to the distressed horses.

When daylight came, they loaded the supplies on the sled and laboriously made their way back to the cabin. Jessie taught the children at home for two weeks, when a crust formed on the snow hard enough to walk on. On arriving back at the school, they found that the snow had drifted up to the eaves of the building. Jessie wondered what had become of the unfortunate horses. Had they sought shelter somewhere else, or were they frozen to death under the snow? Only time would tell.

The following March I had a melancholy letter from Jessie. Would this term never end? They had had such a terrible winter. Then in a lighter vein she wrote, "Spring has come at last. Beautiful spring! The sun is shining, the snow is melting, and the five dead horses in back of my room have begun to thaw out and stink! If that isn't a sign of spring, what is?"

Dear girl! She'd had a pretty tough assignment, and I felt proud of her for having the fortitude to stay with it. But she'd had enough of school teaching for awhile, and she came back home and married her high school sweetheart.

Alice received her teacher's certificate the following year, and joined the teaching staff. She taught one year, and then married Fred, a cowboy sweetheart, that she'd ridden the range with many times. She was fully aware of the fact that there was never a cowboy that could support a family on a cowboy's wages, so after they were married she went right on teaching, and as the storybook goes, "They lived happily ever after."

My friends all laughed and said, "What good did it do you to deprive yourself to educate the girls, just to have them teach one year and get married?" But I didn't feel this way. I felt confident that they were better fitted to raise their families after having had an education than they would have been otherwise.

Twenty-Two

By 1931 our children were all married and gone, and Daddy and I were left alone on the ranch and had been wandering around in our seven-room house, after having raised six children in three rooms. Daddy's health had failed steadily, and he had been bedfast for the last year. I spent all my time caring for him, as we had a man hired to do the ranch work.

Finally we decided to sell out and move to an apartment in Reno, while I looked for a new location. We had been there a very short time when Daddy quietly passed away. He was sitting on the edge of his bed, pillowing his head in my lap, and he had one arm around my neck. He looked up at me with the sweetest smile on his face and said, "Good-bye, old lady. I'm gone."

There was nothing really sad about his passing, for when death comes as a relief to suffering it is a blessing to all concerned.

I was left financially secure, for all our cash was in the bank in my name. Daddy had insisted on it being that way, so that when he was gone there would be no estate to settle.

In 1931, when banks all over the United States closed their doors, there were only two in Nevada that remained open. My little bank account, everything I had in the world in the way of material possessions, was in one of those two banks.

I bought a home in the outskirts of Reno that was easily accessible for visits from my children, grandchildren, and great-grandchildren. Many's the time we gather and make the rafters ring, the same as we did on the old homestead. As I sit here now, in my modest little home, in comfort, and in ample supply, I often spend my time in reminiscing and in looking back over the years, yes, hard years, but full and happy too, it seems a very short time back to that bright, spring morning a half century ago, when Daddy and I with our little flock went homesteading on Tule Mountain and robbed the children's ten-cent banks for our first bill of grub.

Sarah Elizabeth Olds was born in Iowa in 1875, the youngest daughter in a family of ten. Her father, Alexander Thompson, had migrated from Scotland to Canada where he met and married Mary Anne Harper, a recent migrant from Ireland. They settled on a farm near Ottumwa, Iowa.

Spurred by tales of her brother's adventures, Sarah moved to California in 1897, settling in the town of Stent, some eight miles southwest of Sonora.

There she met and married Albert J. Olds, a miner and a member of a distinguished California family. In 1908, after living in Reno for two years, the family moved to a desert homestead about thirty miles north of town.

In 1931 the family moved back to Reno, where Albert soon died. Sarah, her later years devoted to traveling and revising this account of her Nevada homestead, died in 1963, at the age of 88.